THE RICH

WORK

AND

THE POOR

WORK

CONTENT

ACKNOWLEDGMENT

We acknowledge our heavenly Father for making us vessels through which the world can touch Him.

INTRODUCTION

Philippians 2:12

My beloved ones, just like you've always listened to everything I've taught you in the past, I'm asking you now to keep following my instructions as though I were right there with you. Now you must continue to make this new life fully manifested **as you** *live* in the holy awe of God—which brings you trembling into his presence. (TPT)

The meaning of the word **"live"** as represented in the footnote of this scripture in the passion translation reads;

2:12 *The Aramaic can be translated "push through the service of your life" or **"work the work of your life."***

Therefore we can conclude that to live means to push through the service of your life, or to work the work of your life.

Everyone on planet earth is working, but the big question is "how is your work qualified?' Is it *rich* or is it *poor*? A truthful answer to this question will open us up to the reality of what goes on behind the scenes of our individual lives.

The decadence of this earth has made it crucial for us to begin to analyze the service of our lives. How are you serving life? Rich work is productive in that it adds to the value of humanity while poor work diminishes our value and is unproductive. Which one do you engage in everyday?

Money has taken over as god in many Christian lives much to earth's dismay. If the service you render the world is detrimental to spiritual well-being, then I announce to you that your work is a poor one. If you render a service that makes the world spiritually sick and go deeper in spiritual agony, then it is time to drop it and start doing God's rich work.

A popular Nigerian musician recently announced his retirement from singing. He did approve of the way his little daughter was dancing seductively and needed to take time off to train her properly.

That is the consequence of poor work. It will always boomerang. I am happy for him. But how about the many other songs and obscene videos that he produced previously? They have wrecked many lives and are still causing havoc in our overall spiritual well-being.

Why do I refer to an unbeliever in a Christian book, you may ask? It's because many Christian homes still find these lewd music videos entertaining and enjoyable. Our children hardly know the difference between worldliness and godliness as they watch their parents dance and sing to these secular content. The Church reeks of youths with lazy and get-rich-quick mindsets that have never known the value of work because they have never been taught. Is this really what God intended from the beginning?

Your riches do not make you productive. Only your positive impact is counted as productive. The reason many rich people can hardly sleep well at night is because their riches are derived from poor work. The consequences of poor work are adverse and is the reason we have countless wealthy and yet suicidal people on earth, and even in Church.

God's very first commandment to man was to till the earth (Genesis 2). However, man lost the gift of work after humanity disobeyed God by eating of the tree of knowledge. That is why work seems strange to the carnal man.

Right now everyone is working, but mostly for self. The focus of our work determines its ultimate quality. If the focus of my work is God, then my work is rich. On the contrary, if the focus of my work is self, it is considered poor.

After the fall, man started serving self and left God completely. Rich work is spiritual and is designed by God to sustain our spirit man. The time has come to start engaging in the work that is meant to keep us truly alive, our Father's work.

There are three major entities involved in this issue of work;

1. God
2. Man
3. The devil

God is in charge of rich work, while the devil runs poor work. Man is simply caught in between. Our everyday choices reflect the quality of our work and ultimately our lives.

"The Rich Work and The Poor Work" is here to draw the line clearly between productive and unproductive work. These three entities involved in work will be discussed in-depth, dealing with misconceptions concerning each one of them and proffering answers to age-long questions about work.

As you turn the following pages, please have an open heart and allow God directly speak to your soul. Let us begin!

THE ORIGIN OF WORK

Where did this whole concept of work start from? Who introduced work to man and what are the grounds for working? We will answer these questions starting from the beginning of beginnings.

Genesis 2:1

THUS THE heavens and the earth were **finished,** *and all the host of them. (AMP)*

Let's take note of the word, "finished". After Jesus was nailed on the cross, what were His last words?

John 19:30

When Jesus had received the sour wine, He said, **It is finished!** *And He bowed His head and gave up His spirit. (AMP)*

In two places we find the word "finished", not uttered by any human being but by God Almighty Himself. Let's go on.

Genesis 2:2-3

And on the seventh day God ended His work which He had done; and He rested on the seventh day from all His work which He had done. And God blessed (spoke good of) the seventh day, set it apart as His own, and hallowed it, because on it God rested from all

His work which He had created and done.

(AMP)

After the work, God blessed. So the blessing is already upon everything He created. The Lord rested on the seventh-day and blessed it. Invariably the sixth, fifth, fourth up till the first day is summed up in this blessing.

Genesis 2:4

This is the history of the heavens and of the

earth when they were created. In the day that

the Lord God made the earth and the heavens--

(AMP)

I want all of us to note something. You can find the entire Bible from the book of Genesis to Revelation in the second chapter of Genesis.

Genesis 2:5

When no plant of the field was yet in the earth and no herb of the field had yet sprung up, for the Lord God had not [yet] caused it to rain upon the earth and there was no man to till the ground, (AMP)

"When no plant had sprung up?" I thought God said He had finished? I thought we were told in verse 1 that everything was complete? Why is verse 5 telling us something else?

No plant had yet sprung up. This means that indeed, plants were actually created in verse 1 but somebody was meant to do something for it to **spring up!**

The Lord told me on the morning I received this book, to bless his children (workers at Watchmaidens Head office). I blessed them accordingly and the blessing is already resting upon them; but there is an added task that must the carried out for the blessing to **spring up!**

A good depiction of the kind of task that must be carried out for the blessing to spring up is in the testimony of one of my sons. The Lord told me that His hand was already resting upon this son of mine, but he lacked one thing, the grace to give sacrificially. Interestingly, he actually is an ardent giver and gives generously but only to members of his nuclear and extended family.

Nevertheless, the demand of the Lord upon him was to open his heart to people that are not related to him. At this point he was unconsciously limiting the blessings of God in his life by restricting his giving to just his family. He knew his own family but forgot that everyone that is on earth belongs to his Heavenly Father. For the blessing to spread out in mind-blowing proportions, he had to perform the task of expanding the coast of his generosity.

Luke 6:33

And if you are kind and good and do favors to and benefit those who are kind and good and do favors to and benefit you, what quality of credit and thanks is that to you? For even the preeminently sinful do the same. (AMP)

Father Abraham extended his generosity beyond his immediate family and we are all partakers of his blessings today.

In Genesis 2:5 the Lord had not yet caused it to rain upon the earth, meaning He would still get to that. But then again not only rain would cause the earth to produce herbs, God also needed man. He needed man in the beginning and will forever require the cooperation of man to till the earth for produce to spring up.

After the blessing, God needed two things namely;

1. Rain

2. Man

The rain is provided by God Himself (Genesis 2:5) but the man must also work so that the plants and herbs of the field would spring up. Otherwise, the rain will still be of no effect even when it comes down.

Does this sound familiar? Haven't you ever wondered why God's promises seem untrue? Many children of God have neglected their original duty to work. Even when God blesses, we still have our parts to play. When God blesses a man with a job for example, he must still wake up, dress up and show up at work.

As soon as rain hits the earth, weeds also start to spring up. Hence the need for man to be ready to work, because he must remove the weeds that choke the plants that spring up.

Invariably, in our walk with God we must be alert, ready to weed out everything that attempts to choke God's blessings upon our lives. Remember the parable of the seed sower.

Matthew 13:22

As for what was sown among thorns, this is he who hears the Word, but the cares of the world and the pleasure and delight and glamour and deceitfulness of riches **choke** *and suffocate the Word, and it yields no fruit.*
(AMP)

The Bible is so rich in light and relatable to our everyday life if our hearts are open to receive it. Just as man must work to prevent the weeds from choking the plants in

Genesis, he must similarly work to prevent the cares of the world from suffocating God's Word in his heart.

"And there was no man to till the ground" (Genesis 2:5). It is actually when we work that the main thing we see in our lives is what God wants.

Genesis 2:6

But there went up a mist (fog, vapor) from the land and watered the whole surface of the ground-- (AMP)

Is it not so funny that in verse 5, God said that rain needed to come down before the plants could spring up? But He sent vapor from the ground rather than rain from above. To achieve what exactly? It was to prepare the ground for the creation of man. Hallelujah! God needed both the rain and man for the plants and herbs to spring up. He decided to make man first. Why? To work God's work on earth.

God's work will be inoperable if He did not have man to work it. He created everything and it was very good. But He still needed man to work His word for perfection.

Do you see how important you are in God's agenda? If we had a revelation of our assignment on earth, we would be more mindful of our handle on life. God needed to create man to work the word for it to be seen according to his preference.

Genesis 2:7-8

Then the Lord God formed man from the dust of the ground and breathed into his nostrils the breath or spirit of life, and man became a living being. And the Lord God planted a garden toward the east, in Eden [delight]; and there He put the man whom He had formed (framed, constituted). (AMP)

After creating man, God made an abode for him, the Garden in Eden.

Genesis 2:9

And out of the ground the Lord God made to grow every tree that is pleasant to the sight or to be desired--good (suitable, pleasant) for food; the tree of life also in the center of the garden, and the tree of the knowledge of [the difference between] good and evil and blessing and calamity. (AMP)

Do you notice the quantum leap between verse 8 and verse 9? Verse 9 is not like the next day after verse 8. Many years must have spanned between these two verses. Here's why.

Subsequently, God released rain and the man already started working without Eve. We must learn to be imaginative as we read the Bible. As far as many of us are concerned, God made Eve the very next day after creating Adam. Is this even practicable? When we begin to ask God real questions about His Word, He answers. The Holy Spirit will hardly tell you anything until you ask.

I pondered on this scripture and God revealed to me that there was a huge time span between these two events.

Genesis 2:18

GOD said, "It's not good for the Man to be alone; I'll make him a helper, a companion."
(MSG)

The tone of the above verse implies that God had been observing Adam for a long while before concluding that it was not good for him to be alone. Adam had been tilling the earth according to God's mandate, and was definitely enjoying constant fellowship with God in this beautiful Garden. He even named all the animals. Please, could he do all that in one day? Definitely not.

Nevertheless God noticed that he was missing something crucial, Eve.

In Genesis 2:5, the plant and herbs had not yet sprung up. All of a sudden we see a whole new condition; trees had grown and food was now in abundance. This is possible only because somebody had been tilling the ground for a long time. As Adam tilled the ground, the Lord gave rain then the earth yielded an increase.

This is the correct order of things;

1. God releases a blessing.
2. We till the blessing.
3. God sends rain.
4. Then earth yields her increase.

Have you found yourself in a cycle of unfulfilled promises? This is your answer. God originated work and without work, man is but a living corpse.

Prayer Point

Our Heavenly Father we are grateful for this great revelation. Please give us the zeal and passion needed to till our blessings until they come to physical manifestation in Jesus' Mighty Name, Amen

CHAPTER TWO

THE DIVINE NATURE OF WORK

It's so crucial to get busy with the work of our Heavenly Father because, He is the perfect epitome of work. Even in His triune capacity, God is never idle.

As God the Father

Genesis 1:1

In the beginning God created the heavens and the earth. (NKJV)

The very first verse of the entire Bible introduces our Heavenly Father as a workaholic. Please don't be offended by my adoption of the word "workaholic" as a close look at planet earth, will reveal God's nature as an over-achiever. A song writer said; *"God provided oxygen for eight billion people but He put only two people in the garden. Overdose!"*

This is your Father, your provider and the lover of your soul. The one who died for you even while you were yet a sinner. Though the word "workaholic" has a negative connotation according to the wisdom of man, I believe that the entire human vocabulary cannot describe the extent of our Heavenly Father's work.

Wikipedia defines a workaholic as a person who works at the cost of his sleep. If that is the case then our Heavenly Father is guilty as charged, for He never sleeps nor slumbers! (Psalm 121:4). I have always wondered how it must be to be awake from the beginning of age. Epic!

He was so guilty in the eyes of men, that He decided to bear that guilt for the sake of His love for me and died a shameful death to set me free. Please, I would forever be in awe of my maker, whose love for me is unreserved and unrestrained. His love for us is reckless, so is His work ethic. How much could we ever pay, if He were to charge us for the free gift of oxygen? Our God is faithful. Please lets us learn to relax in His finished work. No matter the extent of God's demand upon our lives, we can never outdo Him.

Therefore, working with God is an eternal privilege. Guess what? God even works for humanity as a duty!

Isaiah 64:4

*For from of old no one has heard nor perceived by the ear, nor has the eye seen a God besides You, **Who works** and shows Himself active on behalf of him who [earnestly] waits for Him.*
(AMP)

Let no one deceive you any longer. Work is an expression of love and there is nothing negative about working in line with God's demands.

The Father's focus is work. Nearly all the parables of Jesus, point to God as our Master, and clearly indicate how precious work is to God.

Let's analyze the parable of the wicked husbandmen. (Mark 12:1-12)

Mark 12:1-12

AND [Jesus] started to speak to them in parables [with comparisons and illustrations]. A man planted a vineyard and put a hedge around it and dug a pit for the winepress and built a tower and let it out [for rent] to vinedressers and went into another country. When the season came, he sent a bond servant to the tenants to collect from them some of the fruit of the vineyard. But they took him and beat him and sent him away without anything. Again he sent to them another bond servant, and they stoned him and wounded him in the head and treated him shamefully [sending him away with insults]. And he sent another, and that one they killed; then many others--some they beat, and some they put to death. He had still one left [to send], a beloved son; last of all he sent him to them, saying, They will respect my son. But those tenants said to one another, Here is the heir; come on, let us put him to death, and [then] the inheritance will be ours. And they took him and killed him, and threw [his body] outside the vineyard. Now what will the owner of the vineyard do? He will come and destroy the tenants, and give the vineyard to others. Have you not even read this [passage of] Scripture: The very Stone which [after putting It to the test] the builders rejected has become the Head of the corner [Cornerstone]; This is from the Lord and is His doing, and it is marvelous in our eyes? And they were trying to get hold of Him, but they were afraid of the people, for they knew that He spoke this parable with reference to and against them. So they left Him and departed. (AMP)

A close observation of this scripture will reveal to us that the owner of the vineyard is God the Father. He represents the Master in just about all of Jesus' parables. In the above parable, we popularly point out the following;

- The owner of the vineyard represents God Almighty.
- The vinedressers represent God's children or God's hired hands as the case may be.
- The bond servants that were sent to the tenants characterize prophets of old who were maltreated by God's stiff-necked children (Acts 7:51).
- The reaction of the religious leaders to this parable, and so on.

We usually take note of these bigger issues but fail to recognize the basic fact that the people who God sent messengers to, were working. The vinedressers represent us on earth, working. God has sent several prophets to correct the manner in which we have been working, so as to conform to His own standard, and so that the work would yield positively.

Any work that does not align with God's pattern is an exercise in futility. So God in His infinite mercy is still in the business of sending His servants to the Church, to help His children align with His own dictates. Finally, God sent His son (Jesus) and we killed Him.

If the work we are engaged in is so perfect, why would God need to send people to make amends? We all claim to be active children of God, busy with God's mandate on earth. But are we serving God's purpose or ours?

This is really key because the Lord does not want us to end up cast away on the last day.

*Many will say to Me on that day, Lord, Lord, have we not prophesied in Your name and driven out demons in Your name and done **many mighty works** in Your name? And then I will say to them openly (publicly), I never knew you; depart from Me, you who act wickedly [disregarding My commands]. (AMP)*

This would never be our portion in Jesus' Name. God is more interested in the quality of our work than the quantity. Therefore we must discover His heartbeat concerning work as we pursue His kingdom.

As God the Son

Luke 2:48-49

And when they [Joseph and Mary] saw Him, they were amazed; and His mother said to

Him, Child, why have You treated us like this? Here Your father and I have been anxiously looking for You [distressed and tormented]. And He said to them, How is it that you had to look for Me? Did you not see and know that it is necessary [as a duty] for Me to be in My Father's house and [occupied] about My Father's business? (AMP)

Like Father, like son! The zeal of the Lord was burning in the heart of Jesus even from the young age of twelve.

John 9:4

We must work the works of Him Who sent Me and be busy with His business while it is daylight; night is coming on, when no man can work. (AMP)

When Jesus became of age and started His ministry, he worked round the clock and enjoined His disciples to do same. In the same vein, Jesus is calling upon his bride to get to the business of God's kingdom while it is day. Apart from the linear description of day and night time, there is a deeper meaning which many Christians are hardly aware of. Day time also represents a person's youthful years while night time refers to old age. The best time to get into God's work is when you are young.

One of my daughters entered into full-time ministry at Watchmaidens Ministry at the young age of thirty. She tells us about countless well-meaning friends and family members that consider it a great waste for her to spend her youthful years in ministry. They believe it is wiser to enter full-time ministry in old-age.

How do we expect to get anything meaningful out of kingdom service, when we have this kind of mindset? This is the essence of this book; to expose and correct these debilitating mindsets.

Solomon, the wisest man who ever lived, had this to say about service;

Ecclesiastes 12:1

Honor and enjoy your Creator while you're still young, Before the years take their toll and your vigor wanes, (MSG)

Child of God, learn to give God the best of your life, so that you will enjoy the best of God's hand. Grace to serve God fervently from youthful years is released upon the Church right now in Jesus' Mighty Name, Amen.

John 4:34

Jesus said to them, My food (nourishment) is to do the will (pleasure) of Him Who sent Me and to accomplish and completely finish His work. (AMP)

The work of the Father was food and nourishment to the Son. As followers of Jesus, is this our testimony? Do not be discouraged if you are weak and tired in God's business. Even the disciples found it difficult to wait on Jesus before the Holy Spirit came upon them.

Mark 14:37

And He came back and found them sleeping, and He said to Peter, Simon, are you asleep? Have you not the strength to keep awake and watch [with Me for] one hour? (AMP)

The whole essence of the death and resurrection of Jesus, is the ultimate indwelling of Jesus inside every man, in the person of the Holy Spirit.

As God the Holy Spirit

Acts 4:8

Then Peter, [because he was] filled with [and controlled by] the Holy Spirit, said to them, Rulers of the people and members of the council (the Sanhedrin), (AMP)

The Holy Spirit represents the Spirit of Jesus Christ resident in every child of God. What Jesus could not accomplish as a Being outside of Peter in Mark 14:37, He did inside of him. Hallelujah!

John 16:7

However, I am telling you nothing but the truth when I say it is profitable (good, expedient, advantageous) for you that I go away. Because if I do not go away, the Comforter (Counselor, Helper, Advocate, Intercessor, Strengthener, Standby) will not come to you [into close fellowship with you]; but if I go away, I will send Him to you [to be in close fellowship with you]. (AMP)

The Holy Spirit works full-time as our Counselor, Helper, Advocate, Intercessor, Strengthener and Standby. Now that is a massive workload. I know what it takes for the Holy Spirit to work on my will, emotions and inclinations as an individual. Multiply that by eight billion residents on planet earth. God is amazing!

God is ever busy. We must get busy with His mandate in order to sustain our very existence. We are made in the image and likeness of our Heavenly Father who is ever productive. Therefore, we are wired to be productive. Anything outside productivity will lead to a malfunction. No wonder there are so many malfunctioning Christians. They are hardly working and even when they work, it is mostly unproductive. An end has come to all forms of malfunction as God's children in Jesus' Name.

Acts 1:8

But you shall receive power (ability, efficiency, and might) when the Holy Spirit has come upon you, and you shall be My witnesses in Jerusalem and all Judea and Samaria and to the ends (the very bounds) of the earth. (AMP)

Our attitude to work must be renewed. God's ultimate love language is work, and His side of the equation has long been completed. Now it is up to us to continue His work until His second coming. The equation of our lives thus remains unbalanced, until we get to work

Our job is to be God's witnesses wherever we find ourselves. At work, play, school and so on. Vast opportunities are available if only we are willing.

Prayer Point

Our Heavenly Father we have lost the understanding and importance of work all these years. Please restore us and turn our hearts back to work in Jesus' Mighty Name, Amen.

CHAPTER THREE

THE NEED TO CULTIVATE

Genesis 1:28

And God blessed them and said to them, Be fruitful, multiply, and fill the earth, and subdue it [using all its vast resources in the service of God and man]; and have dominion over the fish of the sea, the birds of the air, and over every living creature that moves upon the earth. (AMP)

Fruitfulness, multiplication, filling the earth and subduing it sound so beautiful. But are you aware that it is a serious mandate that involves hard work? I read a quote on the internet that says *"Being broke is hard; getting rich is hard. Choose your hard."* I really love this quote because it points to the state of the Church today. Do you know that acquiring kingdom wealth is hard work?

All of God's blessings are already created and given but they exist underground. You must till the ground for your blessing to spring up. Apart from material blessings, spiritual gifts like prophecy, healing and even teaching must be tilled to find full expression. This tilling is serious work that we better get busy doing.

Ephesians 2:10

No, we neither make nor save ourselves. God does both the making and saving. He creates each of us by Christ Jesus to join him in the work he does, the good work he has gotten ready for us to do, work we had better be doing. (MSG)

You must till your marriage, your spouse, your children, and your ministry for a harvest to spring up. Many of us have fantastic dreams about God's call upon our lives. We had better start tilling so that God will send His rain of abundance.

The secrets of men are in their stories. When I listen to my Father-in-the-Lord Bishop David Oyedepo, I am more interested in the actions he took to get him to the level he is today. He is a perfect example of the rich work we are meant to be engaged in right now. He has shared with us countless moves he had to make for the earth to yield her increase in Living Faith Church. Days of fasting and seriously seeking God's face in search of revelation. This is the work we had better get busy doing.

God made the heavens and the earth, and said "it is finished". So why does man need to work?

Genesis 2:9-14

*GOD made all kinds of trees grow from the ground, trees beautiful to look at and good to eat. The Tree-of-Life was in the middle of the garden, also the Tree-of-Knowledge-of-Good-and-Evil. A river flows out of Eden to water the garden and from there divides into four rivers. The first is named Pishon; it flows through Havilah where there is **gold.** The gold of this land is good. The land is also known for a sweet-scented resin and the onyx stone. The* *second river is named Gihon; it flows through the land of Cush. The third river is named Hiddekel and flows east of Assyria. The fourth river is the Euphrates. (MSG)*

As man continued tilling, the earth brought forth more treasures like gold and precious stones. We did not see these treasures in verse 1, and even after God had completed creation. We saw them when man started work. Child of God, you carry so much and the world is waiting to see you manifest.

Our Primary Assignment

Matthew 6:9

Pray like this:

'Our Beloved Father, dwelling in the heavenly realms, may the glory of your name be the center on which our lives turn. (TPT)

Every creature has a primary assignment on earth. This assignment is simply to glorify God by being what he has called each one to be. Every other creation of God obeys this simple mandate except man. The sun, moon, stars and the entire galaxy are not doing less than their primary assignment.

The animals, plants and elements are not doing less either. This is why they are always in the right with God.

Matthew 6:26

Look at the birds of the air; they neither sow nor reap nor gather into barns, and yet your heavenly Father keeps feeding them. Are you not worth much more than they? (AMP)

Our primary assignment is to work the ground and keep it in order (Genesis 2:15). How are we fairing?

An airplane for example was created to carry people to desired destinations by air. If it fails to achieve this, it is longer fit to be called an airplane. When a bird ceases to fly, it is no longer a bird.

When humans refuse to work, they are no longer fit to be called humans. Consequently, we have very few true humans on earth. That's the reason the earth is still waiting for the manifestation of the sons of God (Romans 8:19). These ones are the humans that the world is waiting for, to deliver and save them from satan's tyranny.

As God's children, if we find life difficult and it seems like God is not feeding or keeping us, the solution is simple. Let us learn from the birds and get in line with our primary assignment on earth.

What do we see amongst Christians today? A huge number of us have traded work for the pursuit of money. Adam was not paid a dime. He was only asked by God to till and work the earth. How was he paid? The earth yielded her increase. Productivity is a covenant practice, and it does not answer to only prayers. Work the earth and it will yield for you a great harvest. It is that simple.

Genesis 2:15

GOD took the Man and set him down in the Garden of Eden to work the ground and keep it in order. (MSG)

This is where we find our primary assignment. Sometimes people say they don't know why they are created. Let's start from the beginning, tend the garden. Everything God has given to us is a garden. Nigeria is a garden, we must tend it. Anywhere you find yourself right now, the Lord has placed you there to tend.

Worship

Do you realize that the first commandment that God ever gave to man was to tend the garden? (Genesis 2:15). He did not tell man to worship Him, why?

God did not ask man to worship because as we obey Him, we are worshipping. In this part of the world we say countless prayers and sing the most songs. When it is time to act however, we are found wanting.

Worship is you fulfilling purpose. That is, God's purpose for your life, not your own purpose and definitely not another man's own. This is what we must teach our children and youths.

Youths nowadays have become exhausted from praying prayers of vengeance and beggarly cries to God for money. They feel that these kinds of prayers are a chore and a bore, which as a matter of fact, they truly are. They present a false picture of true worship.

How many prayers do birds pray? When Adam was created, how many prayers did he pray? At least we would have been told if there were any prayers he said to God in the morning that made God visit them in the cool of the evening. Nothing of such was mentioned.

Who will teach us how to tend our own fatherland?

Genesis 2:16-17
And the Lord God commanded the man, saying, You may freely eat of every tree of the garden; But of the tree of the knowledge of good and evil and blessing and calamity you

shall not eat, for in the day that you eat of it you shall surely die. (AMP)

Here we find the Lord teaching man how to obey Him. In learning to obey God by tending the earth, it gave man its best (Genesis 2:14). Likewise, the earth will give its worst to hands that refuse to tend it.

Our Homeland

Let us state some facts, some painful realities about our identity in this part of the world. We are all God's children, whether white or black. Therefore, this is far from being racist or sentimental.

In this part of the world, Africa, we sometimes wonder how the white people don't pray as much as we do, yet it seems God is more with them than we Africans who pray tirelessly. The simple explanation is that white people know how to tend the earth. They know how to obey the very first commandment.

Developed countries have hydro geologists whose primary assignment is the study of the distribution and movement of **water** both on and below the Earth's surface, as well as the impact of human activity. Amazing. Over there, you'll see adverts about the proper management of water, but are we interested in this type of thing over here?

They are primarily concerned with ways by which the earth can be preserved for future generations, which is God's first commandment. Is it any surprise that they are doing very well? They came up with the concept of recycling waste. Why? Because the earth is suffering too much.

On the contrary, we are nonchalant about the earth. Once there is a heavy downpour, all drainages get blocked by plastic and nylon materials that could as well be recycled. Then we complain about flood. Seriously? It is time to get busy with God's agenda for the earth.

Do you know that Chinese students attending schools in Canada are always eager to go back to their home country, to be a blessing with their brains? They hardly ever want to stay permanently in Canada. Is it surprising that today, China is the world's largest manufacturing economy and exporter of goods? Meanwhile when our children in Diaspora desire to return to Nigeria, they are met with great opposition and intentional frustration. Many times they shut these children up with political appointments, because they think it is all about money.

God did not give man money. God gave man earth and asked him to till it for Him. If there is anything we should be chasing, it's work not money. That's why someone abroad would be so satisfied making a meagre income as long as he is contributing positively to the society. For him, productivity is not about money but impact.

The average African does not mind living a life of no impact, as long as there is money. This is a great shame. We are constantly building shopping outlets and mansions even up to the point of building on top drainages and pipe lines.

Where are we going? Even if we are leaving this earth, would it not be best to at least leave it the way God made it, without polluting it?

Till your country and it will give you the best. This is God's order of things. How can we expect God's best when we refuse to work His work? He has done His own work; it is time for us to do ours.

We mess up everything including our bodies which are God's temple. Is there anything against going to heaven in perfect health? God's Word says;

Exodus 23:26

There shall nothing cast their young, nor be barren, in thy land: the number of thy days I will fulfil. (KJV)

God's ordained blessing is fulfillment of the number of our days. However, we must actively work out its implications in our lives. We must be responsible for our health, which is our part to play. We must cooperate with God by eating right and exercising our bodies.

Many servants of God are dying too early because they refused to be mindful of their physical health. Shouldn't we learn from their demise? We lack health education in this part of the world and enough is enough! The earth, our bodies, creation as a whole has had enough of our mindlessness.

Adam's Undone Work

Genesis 2:22-23

GOD then used the rib that he had taken from the Man to make Woman and presented her to the Man. The Man said, "Finally! Bone of my bone, flesh of my flesh! Name her Woman for she was made from Man." (MSG)

Adam missed something, he was meant to work Eve and Eve would have given him her increase. But there was no increase to give because Adam never worked Eve. This is deep.

Eve might have looked like a finished product, but she actually was not. She needed to be tilled by Adam to get God's best from her. Consequently, this untilled blessing landed Adam and the whole of humanity in death. Thank God for the saving power of Jesus Christ.

Adam was meant to work Eve, so that the Lord will help her work Adam as well. This is the missing secret in most Christian homes today. Nobody wants to work their spouse. Hence they end up in a cycle of frustration and regret.

How do I work my spouse? By praying him/her into God's will and purpose. Everything that is created is meant to be worked.

Though Jesus said "it is finished" on the cross (John 19:30), we are still told to work out our salvation with fear and trembling (Philippians 2:12).

The Earth as an Entity

Evidence of rich and poor work is everywhere you look. We are even exposed to a deeper understanding in the parables of Jesus. For example, in the parable of the sower, the seeds that were planted had no problem. It was the soils which represent the earth in different forms that had issues (Matthew 13).

The earth refers to the kind of work we do as individuals because we are all made of earth (Genesis 2:7). The work we do, springs out of the depths of our hearts. Hence, the roadside, rocky soil, thorny soil and good soil represent different states of the human heart. The quality of the work I do, whether rich or poor, will reflect in the way the earth (my heart) treats the seed that is planted in it. Deep!

Therefore, the earth is an entity that responds according to the way it is treated.

Have you ever wondered why we have Tsunamis? It's because the location of such Tsunami is most likely deep in Godlessness. Because the earth cannot take it anymore it reacts by vomiting its contents. The earth is a living entity. If this was not so, how then could it reward man with its fruit?

Leviticus 26:34-35

With you gone and dispersed in the countries of your enemies, the land, empty of you, will finally get a break and enjoy its Sabbath years. All the time it's left there empty, the land will get rest, the Sabbaths it never got when you lived there. (MSG)

God has created the earth in such a way that it recycles itself. So it must be left alone to enjoy its rest according to God's instruction.

This scripture above describes a period when the Israelites abused the land and deprived it of its Sabbath rest. They were sent into captivity by God because they abused the earth! This is an extremely serious matter. Is it possible that the many troubles that plague us is as a result of the abuse that earth has received from us? May God have mercy!

The ground of Nigeria is crying seriously because of the innocent blood that has been shed. Any work we engage in that is detrimental to the spiritual and physical well-being of the earth and others is termed poor work. The earth cannot yield positive increase when negative seeds are sown.

One of my daughters who studied Animal Science in Nigeria was told that graduates in Animal science are trained to manage animal ranches. Sadly, Nigerian government, instead of creating an enabling environment for qualified graduates to manage our cattle, prefer to allow herdsmen parade their cattle on the streets thereby threatening the lives of people.

Nigeria used to be so rich in Teak wood and Mahogany for example, but is now importing them from other countries, due to the mismanagement of our God-given resource.

It is crucial to note that the earth represents not just land, but the air as well. When will we repent from polluting God's gift? Christians, it is time to start praying for the earth.

2 Chronicles 7:14
and my people, my God-defined people,
respond by humbling themselves, praying,
seeking my presence, and turning their backs
on their wicked lives, I'll be there ready for

you: I'll listen from heaven, forgive their sins, and restore their land to health. (MSG)

The Need to Work

Exodus 3:17

And I have said, I will bring you up out of the affliction of Egypt unto the land of the Canaanites, and the Hittites, and the Amorites, and the Perizzites, and the Hivites, and the Jebusites, unto a land flowing with milk and honey. (KJV)

God blessed the Israelites with a land flowing with milk and honey with their enemies still residing in the land! This is God's way of training His children.

Therefore, we should not be weary or discouraged when our lives seem so full of battles. They make us stronger and we are actually fighting from a place of victory, not defeat. All we do is reenact the victory Jesus wrought for us on the cross of Calvary.

Work is what keeps man alive, but most believers and most Nations are dying because they are not working. Work kept our fore-fathers alive for many long years. It is time to wake up!

Prayer Point

Heavenly Father, I believe that my eyes will see a new Nigeria and a revived Church, one that is finally awake to her calling by You and is fully engaged in the rich work that You have called us to. So shall it be in Jesus' Mighty Name.

CHAPTER FOUR

RICH WORK; THE HARD TRUTH

2 Corinthians 4:11

We consider living to mean that we are constantly being handed over to death for Jesus' sake so that the life of Jesus will be revealed through our humanity. (TPT)

Work is considered rich only when it is productive. When you decide to be productive, it's like you are actually dying every day because the work is not about you. When you live life and the life is not about you, then it's about something or someone else. A Productive life is all about Christ and that is what the devil stole from man.

Eve decided to live for herself and it led to her great fall. You being productive is therefore you not living for yourself.

I accepted this assignment as a full-time minister of God. I am not living for myself. I was actually doing well before God called me into this. As at the time He called me, I already owned a house, cars, children and every good thing of life, but in the eyes of God I wasn't living a productive life until I started His assignment. Now I'm even happier and ready to answer God's call anytime.

I am giving what He wants me to give to earth. This is rich work. Rich work consists of living by the dictates of God's Word as a lifestyle.

Money is not productivity. If you give money to people as a philanthropist, that is fantastic. However, a nobler deed would be to contribute to the mental and spiritual development of the youths and society at large. We must begin to contribute to helping the youths think right and be positively productive.

When the Lord commanded Adam to work, He meant that he should be productive according to God's prescribed standard of living.

In this kingdom, the work is finished on God's part. All I need to do is to till the finished work. I must be an expression of God's completed work by believing His every Word, both logo (written word) and rhema (personal revelation). I need to get my hands dirty as I dig through the hidden treasures of scripture. No one would do this work for us.

Instances of Rich Work

So far, we have said quite a lot about rich work. Here are some instances that exemplify rich work.

1. EYES TO THE BLIND.

Job 29:15

I was eyes to the blind and feet to the lame,

(MSG)

There are people around you that are blind even though they can see. Rich work is a call to be their eyes.

A family member once came to me asking for financial assistance. This had become her fixed way of life, begging. On this occasion, the Holy Spirit opened my eyes to see that she was blind to her own potential. She had never worked for one day in her entire life, because she just never found anything she was good at.

We discovered however that she speaks very good English, and could start teaching children how to speak, for a small fee. She jumped at the idea and dived into it immediately. From that time till now, she has not begged for money.

2. FEET TO THE LAME.

Job 29:15

I was eyes to the blind and feet to the lame,

(MSG)

Similarly, there are people who have functional legs but they are lame. These people seem so busy, but they are hardly ever productive. When the Lord reveals something to you concerning such people, your assignment is to be their feet. Open your mouth, move, help them in any way you can by suggesting positive ideas to them. Make suggestions that they cannot see, but you can. If you are able to sponsor them financially, go right ahead.

Proverbs 19:17

If you help the poor, you are lending to the LORD- and he will repay you! (NLT)

This is a fantastic kingdom investment opportunity that many of us have ignored for too long. Is this not what makes us Christians? Do not be stingy with godly counsel, it is of no use in heaven anyway.

These are fantastic job opportunities in this kingdom. Rather than criticizing and judging people, be their eyes and feet. Get busy helping people and make it your full time employment. Now you know, dive in!

3. PRAYER.

One thing we must understand about God's work is that He has finished the creative work. Everything is still in seed form, waiting to be tilled and brought forth. No matter how hard we work, our arch enemy will never make it easy to accomplish. Hence the need for constant communion with God in prayer.

Sadly, the concept of prayer has been greatly abused and misunderstood by God's children. Many Christians have turned prayers into vain repetitions just like the heathen.

Prayer is simply communication with God and must be done in truth and in spirit (John 4:24).

Only a handful of God's children understand this and actively pursue God's purpose here on earth. God's ultimate goal is to establish His kingdom here on earth and this cannot be done carnally.

Zechariah 4:6

So he answered and said to me: "This is the word of the LORD to Zerubbabel: 'Not by might nor by power, but by My Spirit,' Says the

LORD of hosts. (NKJV)

Only by God's Spirit through prayer is God's will established here on earth. Every kingdom activity must be backed up by prayer to yield results.

On the other hand, if you pray from morning till night without fulfilling God's purpose for life, nothing will change.

4. FAITH.

The only work that Jesus commanded us to do is to believe.

John 6:28-29

Then they asked him, "What must we do to do the works God requires?" Jesus answered, "The work of God is this: to believe in the one he has sent." (NIV)

Doubt disconnects us from the flow of God's blessings. Let us examine this illustration to explain our work of faith. Imagine a family of four children and two parents who came home from a Church service full of God's Word and ready to begin the new week gloriously. But the next day, they are faced with serious hunger as there is no food to eat. They have a choice either to hold on to the word they heard in Church, about God never forsaking His beloved; or break the flow of their blessing with doubt.

Someone is already on their way to the family with a huge blessing, including the children's school fees, house rent and so on. What sustains its fulfillment and manifestation is holding on to God's Word.

Faith is actually what holds the pipe of blessings and keeps the water flowing.

The fight of faith is a fight of holding on to God's sure Word, and this is rich work. It is a serious fight because we see ourselves having strong faith sometimes and no faith at other times.

However, faith must be backed up by works of obedience.

James 2:26

For as the human body apart from the spirit is lifeless, so faith apart from [its] works of obedience is also dead. (AMP)

5. PATIENCE.

The Lord once said to me that without patience, I can never work with Him. I have come to realize that impatience with God is pointless because I don't even know the way, neither can I give any blessing to myself.

Imagine that you booked a flight ticket to Abuja from Lagos for instance, and the flight gets delayed for about five hours. You will learn patience naturally; except you want to enter the air by yourself and take yourself to Abuja.

We are happy and waiting patiently when our earthly flight is delayed. Why is it so hard to have the same patient disposition towards God and His Word? Hence, patience is key in carrying out exploits in this kingdom.

Thomas Edison who invented the light bulb tried and failed one thousand times before succeeding. Now the world is enjoying the outcome of his rich and patient work. The same thing applies to other great inventors on earth. Long after their death, the world is still enjoying their hand work.

We need to cultivate the habit of patience that we see in the lives of Bible patriarchs. Examples are Job, Joseph, King David, Abraham and many others. Even Jesus came 4,000 years after it was prophesied.

When you decide to live a life of patience, faith and prayer, you will discover spiritual growth and maturity.

What made Eve eat the forbidden fruit? Impatience. From the very beginning, humanity has struggled with this virtue.

Faith without patience is not balanced. Faith and patience are parts of the fruit of the Spirit mentioned in Galatians 5:22-23. They need to be nurtured in us for us to bear fruits that will abide.

Patience is the ultimate test of our faith and trust in God's timing. Do you get angry and agitated when things are not going your way? The fruit of patience must grow and keep growing for rich work to be made manifest in our lives.

Some of us can wait on God for one, two or three years, but can we wait twenty years?

The right attitude of patience is to keep working while we wait; and keep thanking God constantly for answering our prayers.

Philippians 4:6

Do not fret or have any anxiety about anything, but in every circumstance and in everything, by prayer and petition (definite requests), with thanksgiving, continue to make your wants known to God. (AMP)

Sadly, the blessings of Matthew 6:33 have been eluding Christians because they cannot wait till the end. It takes maturity to wait on God for food, shelter and clothing. We have been having things our own way like the people of the world.

1 Peter 4:1

Since Jesus went through everything you're going through and more, learn to think like him. Think of your sufferings as a weaning from that old sinful habit of always expecting to get your own way. (MSG)

It is time to get up.

Benefits of Rich Work

Let us point out some resultant effects of engaging actively in rich work.

1. DISTASTE FOR SIN.

Many Christians still struggle with sin because they have not found solid footing in our Father's kingdom business. One of my daughters who was an active masturbator, lesbian and drug addict has lost taste for those former desires. Now, she tells me that her new high is the Holy Spirit. Because rich work is focused on God, there is hardly any chance to gratify the lustful desires of the flesh!

Galatians 5:16

But I say, walk and live [habitually] in the [Holy] Spirit [responsive to and controlled and guided by the Spirit]; then you will certainly not gratify the cravings and desires of the flesh (of human nature without God). (AMP)

Do you find yourself still struggling with an impossible addiction? Then get engaged in the rich work that God is calling all His children into. Our walk with God is a journey. The more you engage with God, your taste for sin becomes lesser and lesser. Temptations come and defeat so many Christians because they are not working.

Jesus was so busy working that temptations could not overpower Him and the enemy could not find anything in Him.

John 14:30

I will not talk with you much more, for the prince (evil genius, ruler) of the world is coming. And he has no claim on Me. [He has nothing in common with Me; there is nothing in Me that belongs to him, and he has no power over Me.] (AMP)

You can never be trapped by sin if you are neck deep in our heavenly Father's business, in truth and in spirit. The grace to serve diligently is released afresh upon the Church in Jesus' Mighty Name, Amen.

2. GOD'S PRESENCE.

Matthew 6:33

But seek (aim at and strive after) first of all His kingdom and His righteousness (His way of doing and being right), and then all these things taken together will be given you besides. (KJV)

Matthew 6:33 for me means that if I make up my mind to fulfill God's purpose for my life, He follows me just like He followed Adam and Eve.

Genesis 3:8a

And they heard the sound of the Lord God walking in the garden in the cool of the day... (AMP)

It was God's practice to visit Adam and Eve in the cool of the day, perhaps after the day's work had ended. Therefore actively pursuing the interest of God's kingdom in the form of rich work keeps God presence with you all your life! And it is God's presence that attracts everything that is good to you. This work that is called rich, actually separates you from the world. It draws you closer and closer into the presence of the Father. You keep getting stronger. Your joy is attacked but never taken. You are persecuted but not destroyed. You are mocked, yet you keep working and you have a strange peace that baffles the world. It is a beautiful place to be, in rich service.

3. RICH BLESSINGS.

Ephesians 1:3

May blessing (praise, laudation, and eulogy) be to the God and Father of our Lord Jesus Christ (the Messiah) Who has blessed us in Christ with every spiritual (given by the Holy Spirit) blessing in the heavenly realm! (AMP)

Engaging fully in rich work, causes you to experience every spiritual blessing in the heavenly realm that is already ours for the taking. Rich work unlocks the treasury of God's blessings upon the life of every believer.

4. FRUITFULNESS.

Rick work empowers the redeemed for fruitfulness.

Exodus 23:25-26

"But you--you serve your GOD and he'll bless your food and your water. I'll get rid of the sickness among you; there won't be any miscarriages nor barren women in your land. I'll make sure you live full and complete lives.
(MSG)

In addition, they shall have the capacity to keep bearing fruit till old age

Psalm 92:13-14

Planted in the house of the Lord, they shall flourish in the courts of our God. [Growing in grace] they shall still bring forth fruit in old age; they shall be full of sap [of spiritual vitality] and [rich in the]

verdure [of trust, love, and

contentment]. (AMP)

5. YOU EARN YOUR PAY.

God pays his laborers their due wages.

1 Corinthians 3:8

He who plants and he who waters are equal

(one in aim, of the same importance and

esteem), yet each shall receive his own reward

(wages), according to his own labor. (AMP)

Requirements for Rich Work

1. HAVE A JOYFUL HEART.

Joy and rejoicing must accompany our work for it to be rich.

Joel 1:12

Vineyards dried up, fig trees withered,

Pomegranates, date palms, and apple trees--

deadwood everywhere! **And joy is dried up**

and withered in the hearts of the people.

(MSG)

Joy is dried up in many service units today in the Church, and this is why there are no rewards for many.

Deuteronomy 28:47-48

Because you didn't serve GOD, your God, out of

the joy and goodness of your heart in the great

abundance, you'll have to serve your enemies

whom GOD will send against you. Life will be

famine and drought, rags and wretchedness;
then he'll put an iron yoke on your neck until
he's destroyed you. (MSG)

It is better not to serve at all than to give a joyless service.

2. QUIT COMPLAINING.

Numbers 11:1

The people fell to grumbling over their hard life. GOD heard. When he heard his anger flared; then fire blazed up and burned the outer boundaries of the camp. (MSG)

Why invest in what does not work? What has ever come out of complaining? Let go of sorrow of heart and begin to see God's hand. Paul and Silas sang their way out of trouble (Acts 16:25). Your complaint over your business is what is killing it.

3. AVOID JOY BREAKERS.

1 Samuel 1:17-18

Then Eli said, Go in peace, and may the God of Israel grant your petition which you have asked of Him. Hannah said, Let your handmaid find grace in your sight. So [she] went her way and ate, her countenance no longer sad. (AMP)

Stay away from joy breakers. They are destiny robbers

4. BE RESPONSIBLE.

2 Timothy 1:6

Therefore I remind you to stir up the gift of God which is in you through the laying on of my hands. (NKJV)

Search out your faith and let God rewrite your story. God can only work to the extent that your faith is stirred

5. REMAIN COMMITED.

Proverbs 14:23

Hard work always pays off; mere talk puts no bread on the table. (MSG)

Talk is cheap. Get busy and quit idle talks.

6. BE RIGHTLY POSITIONED.

Proverbs 13:20

He who walks with wise men will be wise, But the companion of fools will be destroyed.
(NKJV)

God is no respecter of persons. He is not shy with His gifts, but many of His children are not yielding to His call. This lack of yielding is what makes it look like God is not working.

There are some positions however, that you place yourself in life that will make you yield to God unfailingly. Bishop David Oyedepo always says, "The Company you keep, *determines what accompanies you in life."* Surround yourself with those on the same wavelength with you and see yourself soar higher and higher, beyond the level you would have ever attained alone.

I pray that the Lord will bring every child of God to that position where we are able to yield to Him. In Jesus' Name. Amen.

7. CHECK THE CHASE.

Matthew 6:33

*"So above all, **constantly** seek God's kingdom and his righteousness, then all these less important things will be given to you abundantly. (TPT)*

The heart is always constantly chasing after something per time whether we are aware of it or not. You might even be a serious Church-goer but with a heart that is chasing something other than God. A good example is Judas Iscariot. He was always with God Almighty in the person of Jesus but his heart constantly chased after money.

Every time I ignore God, He is not the one I am chasing anymore, and He is no longer my focus at that point. This can be within a spilt second, so It is our duty to check the chase of our hearts every time.

8. BE ADDICTED TO CELEBRATING GOD.

Psalm 34:1

I bless GOD every chance I get; my lungs expand with his praise. (MSG)

Here are three things that made Abraham an epitome of God's favor;

1. He was in love with God. Be in love with God. When you love what God loves, all things keep working together for your good. (Romans 8:28; Isaiah 41:8; James 2:23; Psalm 105:42). God wants all men saved, and Abraham also interceded for Sodom and Gomorrah in line with God's mandate and passion for souls.

2. He served God earnestly.

Genesis 12:1&4

NOW [in Haran] the Lord said to Abram, Go for yourself [for your own advantage] away from your country, from your relatives and your father's house, to the land that I will show you. So Abram departed, as the Lord had directed him; and Lot [his nephew] went with him.

Abram was seventy-five years old when he left Haran. (AMP)

Even in old age, Abraham obeyed and served God earnestly.

3. He was strong in faith.

Romans 4:19-20

Abraham didn't focus on his own impotence and say, "It's hopeless. This hundred-year-old body could never father a child." Nor did he survey Sarah's decades of infertility and give up. He didn't tiptoe around God's promise asking cautiously skeptical questions. He plunged into the promise and came up strong, ready for God, (MSG)

If we claim to be Abraham's seed, then we must do his work.

Prayer Point

Heavenly Father, we have heard Your word today. However, we will never be able to execute it without Your help. This we pray earnestly for and receive with gratitude in Jesus' precious Name. Amen.

CHAPTER FIVE

POOR WORK DEFINED

Any work that is detrimental to the spiritual and mental well-being of people can be classified as poor work. For example, the worldly entertainment industry is making so much money, but they are keenly engaged in poor work. After consuming all the goods that they have to offer humanity, victims end up either suicidal or spiritually contaminated with sin. Poor work.

Even secular musicians do not want their children to be contaminated by worldliness. The focus of poor work is purely money. It has no concern for the well-being of humanity as long as it brings in money.

If you are destroying human beings, you are not productive. The devil himself is working but is he productive? Think about it.

Our world is messed up today, because we have been giving it poor work. Many Christians cannot even be distinguished from unbelievers in their places of work. They are drawn deeper and deeper into the ways of the world and it is really sad.

Instances of Poor Work

For a very long time, the Children of God have imbibed very poor work ethics as their lifestyle. How can we handle our Heavenly Father's business shabbily and expect glorious lives? The quality of the life of every believer is directly proportional to his/her attitude to God's work. Here are some instances that typify poor work.

1. THE BLAME GAME.

This is one of the most subtle tricks of the enemy. It is the very first self-defeating game that our parents, Adam and Eve played. Adam went as far as blaming God. Just like Adam, many Christians inwardly blame God for their unwanted predicaments. Here's what the scripture says about blaming God;

Proverbs 19:3

People ruin their lives by their own stupidity,

so why does GOD always get blamed? (MSG)

No one is to be blamed for your predicament. Anywhere you find blame, you find irresponsibility right next to it.

Furthermore many of us go to the other extreme, this time blaming the devil. Christians don't wake up early and get to the business of the day, it is the devil. They wake up late, get to work late and get fired, it is the devil. If the devil is so powerful, why did he not stop us from eating?

Any faith that makes God solely responsible for the fulfillment of His will on earth, is an irresponsible faith. God's true children always take responsibility for their actions and are readily repentant like King David (Psalm 51).

Jesus, the last Adam has changed the course of irresponsibility and taught us how to quit the blame game. It only keeps us far away from God and makes us constantly joyless.

John 9:3

Jesus said, "You're asking the wrong question. You're looking for someone to blame. There is no such cause-effect here. Look instead for what God can do. (MSG)

Our old nature is always looking for someone to blame. This is poor and unproductive.

2. VANITY.

Revelation 2:20

"But why do you let that Jezebel who calls herself a prophet mislead my dear servants into Cross-denying, self-indulging religion? (MSG)

Is this not the reality of many believers today? Vanity is self-indulgent and cross denying. This is poor work. Anytime we find ourselves more focused on physical appearance than God's passion, we have entered vanity.

Psalm 4:2

*O you sons of men, how long will you turn my honor and glory into shame? How long will you love **vanity and futility** and seek after lies? Selah [pause, and calmly think of that]! (AMP)*

We hardly seek after the truth anymore. All we are mostly interested in is prophesies that massage our egos. No wonder most believers are void of God's power.

3. IDOLATRY.

1 Corinthians 10:7

And do not become idolaters as were some of them. As it is written, "The people sat down to eat and drink, and rose up to play." (NKJV)

An idol is anything that takes the place of God in our lives. The propelling force of idolatry is self. Whereas money and possessions have no power to become our idols, it is man that installs these objects in his heart and makes idols of them.

Idolatry is an instance of poor work that has led many people to early graves.

It is time to turn to God and cry for mercy.

Psalm 119:37

Turn away my eyes from beholding vanity (idols and idolatry); and restore me to vigorous life and health in Your ways. (AMP)

Prayer Point

Father in the Name of Jesus, please renew our minds and cause us to be productive in Your own way. In Jesus' Mighty Name. Amen.

CHAPTER SIX

RICH WORK VERSUS POOR WORK

The overall productivity of your work determines if it is rich or poor.

Oxford dictionary defines productivity as;

"the effectiveness of productive effort, especially in industry, as measured in terms of the rate of output per unit of input".

How many Christians are interested in *industry* anymore? Statistics today show that the Nigerian manufacturing sector contributes less than ten percent (10%) to our Gross Domestic Product.

Rather than improving our manufacturing sector, our youths are now fully engaged in other business ventures like bit coin, sports betting and internet fraud. They hardly want to learn any trade or contribute to their own posterity. What have believers done about this so far?

Someone might say. *"But I am working hard. I wake up every morning, go to work and actively till every day. My bank account is fat and my body is not idle. You can't tell me that I am engaged in poor work"*.

Oxford dictionary defines work as;

"Activity involving mental or physical effort done in order to achieve a purpose or result".

"A task or tasks to be undertaken".

A task that is to be undertaken represents something that has been given to you to do in order to achieve a purpose or result. Before you can determine whether your work is rich or poor, you must be able to answer this question;

"What purpose and what result is my work meant to achieve?"

When I look at secular Nigerian artists, their purpose and results are driven by money. Their focus is simply how to make more money. People like them would do anything to make money.

It is not news that the millions of views on these secular songs are contributed by many acclaimed Christians. These music videos are played so comfortably and non-stop in millions of Christian homes. Therefore, we might as well talk about it here since the aim of this book is for Christians to be delivered.

Someone might say *"Why are you saying that a worldly Nigerian artists' work is poor? He is beneficial to me, because he helps me to relax."*

Let's tell ourselves the truth. These songs and movies do not help anyone relax. They are just entertainment we are used to and simply decide to continue "enjoying".

Ecclesiastes 9:10b

... For there's neither work to do nor thoughts to think In the company of the dead, where you're most certainly headed. (MSG)

If indeed it helps you relax, how come you get to a particular point in your life and begin to hate the songs? What happened? It is all about believing this same lie of the enemy that makes excuses to pollute the spirit man.

Get this right. Carnal songs are not helping you in any way, neither are they helping your children. They are injurious to your spirit man.

Interestingly, though these guys engage in poor work, they are the ones that the government recognize and brand ambassadors. Isn't this an anomaly? Why do Christians keep allowing things like this to go on, then go complaining and murmuring under our breaths about the "state of the nation"? Enough is enough!

Luke 16:8

And [his] master praised the dishonest (unjust) manager for acting shrewdly and prudently; for the sons of this age are shrewder and more prudent and wiser in [relation to] their own generation [to their own age and kind] than are the sons of light. (AMP)

It is time to rise up to our responsibilities as sons of light in this generation. Why complain about unbelievers being our nation's brand ambassadors? They are active and alive to their responsibilities. They do not shy away when a representative is needed to stand in for the nation. Where are the Christians? This book is not for unbelievers, but for believers to wake up. We are the ones that would fix the earth that our heavenly Father created.

An unbeliever would not go and read Genesis 2 for me, I'm the one who is meant to read it up and discover what God says I am missing. Thereafter, it is my responsibility to correct my thoughts, not any unbeliever.

We refer to non-believing Nigerian artists because sadly, many Christians have reduced themselves to chasing money like them. This teaching is not for unbelievers. They can chase whatever the world offers and God would not count it against them because they have chosen their path. However, there is a problem when the body of Christ is actively doing the same things as unbelievers. So who is going to stand in the gap for the redemption of earth?

Exodus 36:2

Moses summoned Bezalel and Oholiab along with all whom GOD had gifted with the ability to work skillfully with their hands. The men were eager to get started and engage in the work. (MSG)

Only a handful of our youths are eager to get busy with rich and productive work. It is quite sad. However this is also the time for a great harvest of souls. Many of these youth are eager to hear God's pure Word. Will you partner with God to save their lives and ultimately the life of this nation?

Enugu state in Nigeria, used to be all about mining. The Enugu Coal Region covers 270,000 hectares of the coal basin. It has contributed the largest amount of commercial mining in the past. But what has it become nowadays? This great resource is one of the many good things that God created in Genesis 2. However, youths find it uncool to engage in mining because it doesn't produce quick riches.

Proverbs 13:11

Wealth [not earned but] won in haste or unjustly or from the production of things for vain or detrimental use [such riches] will dwindle away, but he who gathers little by little will increase [his riches]. (AMP)

Our youth have hardly ever learned how to gather little by little. I always tell my sons never to depend on the wealth of their biological father. Any child that wastes years trying to get rich quick, ends up toiling in old age. Every day we see many examples of elderly men laboring as bricklayers and construction workers. It is obvious that their youth was spent carelessly chasing after the wind.

The Ice-Breaker

The major thing that distinguishes rich work from poor work is the spirit behind it. Have you ever experienced watching movies that have pure and moral depictions, but you ended up having nightmares because of them? That explains it. Once it is detrimental to your spirit man, it is a poor work and must be stopped before it kills you the perpetrator.

Galatians 6:7-8

Don't be misled: No one makes a fool of God. What a person plants, he will harvest. The person who plants selfishness, ignoring the needs of others--ignoring God!- harvests a crop of weeds. All he'll have to show for his life is weeds! But the one who plants in response to God, letting God's Spirit do the growth work in him, harvests a crop of real life, eternal life.
(MSG)

Poor work drains the spirit man. Once the spirit man is drained, the physical body will feel it too. That's why people who engage in poor work are always tired, exhausted and yawning endlessly. When they sit down to assess work done, they realize that they actually have done little to nothing. Why are they always tired and stressed? It is poor work.

On the other hand, rich work energizes, restores, revives and refreshes the spirit man. People who engage in rich work are always excited, happy and full of energy. All they need is a minimum amount of rest and afterwards they jump into the work again. It is fulfilling.

Prayer Point

Father in the Name of Jesus, please channel our minds to the truth of Your Word. Help us to seek only the pure truth of Your Word and embrace it always. In Jesus most precious Name we pray, Amen.

CHAPTER SEVEN

WORK VERSUS MONEY

The earth blessed Adam, not money. In those days there was no money to quantify Adam's wealth. So would you say he was a poor man? Certainly not. Do we see how the enemy has used money to blind us from living productive lives?

Everyone is now chasing money, both parents and children alike. Everyone is chasing money, not work. The struggle is fierce because this is God's commandment. Anything that is God's commandment is usually fought against by the kingdom of darkness.

Have you ever seen work as God's commandment? God made me understand this fact; **_"until you work it, it does not work."_** God has blessed humanity and the earth, but we must work it out. It is essential to work out these blessings because all of them are here on earth. They are not in heaven because they are not needed there.

Rather than work, we are busy chasing money. And it is this same money that has been killing many children of God. Adam lived a very long and full life in the absence of money. Is this not enough proof that money is killing us in our time? Why would you kidnap someone and ask someone else to give to you money? Money is killing you.

Which bank did our Father Abraham own? In Genesis 12, God promised Abraham a new land. Making use of land involves many kinds of work. Therefore the gift of land restates the fact that work is a critical scope of God's agenda for man. Abraham was called blessed because he was ready to work.

If you refuse to work, the earth will not yield its increase. It is time to release that song, that book, that project, that hidden treasure that the world is waiting for. There is no better time than right now. Receive the grace for glorious execution in Jesus' Mighty Name, Amen.

Understanding Money

Ecclesiastes 10:19

A feast is made for laughter, and wine maketh merry: but money answereth all [things]. (KJV)

This Scripture has long been greatly misunderstood as meaning that money calls the shorts in our lives.

A closer look at this Scripture reveals the fact that money answers to things, meaning that money is designed by God to answer to all things when called upon. Just like a humble servant.

Money is an entity, a servant that answers when we call upon it as its master. Just as a servant faithfully serves his master, money is created to serve you. However money only answers when God is in it.

If I had a headache for example, money will answer and get me medicine; but money would not give me healing. It is God that would heal me. Money has no capacity to heal me because it is not God. This is evident in the fact that many rich people still end up dying of strange diseases in spite of the millions in their bank accounts.

God did not create money, Man did. How can it be that the thing we created to serve us has now become our master?

The money in my bank account is meant to serve me. But all of a sudden, when I keep the money and start bowing to it by certain actions that I take and the decisions I make, it is obvious that I am now worshipping money.

Therefore, things now answer to money in my life, instead of money answering to things. Money has now become master in the lives of God's children. The reason is because that is all majority of us chase. Whatever I chase is my master and my treasure.

Matthew 6:21

For where your treasure is, there will your heart be also. (AMP)

Once I chase money and make it my master, it becomes my god and it controls everything that concerns me. It determines my mood, my countenance, when I eat, what I wear and so on. Is this not the sad state of countless believers today?

The good news is that there are also quite a few Christians who are masters over money just like our Master, Jesus.

How Jesus Handled Money

Matthew 17:24-27

When they arrived at Capernaum, the tax men came to Peter and asked, "Does your teacher pay taxes?" Peter said, "Of course." But as soon as they were in the house, Jesus confronted him. "Simon, what do you think? When a king levies taxes, who pays--his children or his subjects?" He answered, "His subjects." Jesus said, "Then the children get off free, right? But so we don't upset them needlessly, go down to the lake, cast a hook, and pull in the first fish that bites. Open its mouth and you'll find a coin. Take it and give it to the tax men. It will be enough for both of us." (MSG)

Our Master, the Lord of all, could never be trapped by money. He was in charge of money such that money answered when He called for it. This is the perfect example of our expected attitude towards money. When Jesus needed to pay His taxes, He simply called it forth from the mouth of a fish! Such class!

Let's examine another scripture that reveals Christ's mind-set about money;

John 6:5-7

As Jesus sat down, he looked out and saw the massive crowd of people scrambling up the hill, for they wanted to be near him. So he turned to Philip and said, "Where will we buy enough food to feed all these people?" Now Jesus already knew what he was about to do, but he said this to stretch Philip's faith.

Philip answered, "Well, I suppose if we were to give everyone only a snack, it would cost

thousands of dollars to buy enough food!"
(TPT)

Similarly, Jesus always knows how to meet our needs, but would allow certain tough situations in our lives to stretch our faith. Here's what the footnote of that scripture says;

"two hundred pieces of silver." This equates to about eight months' wages of the average person. Philip didn't answer the question and was focused on how much money it would cost, but Jesus' question was, "Where will we buy bread?" Jesus was testing Philip to see if he would look to Jesus to supply all that was needed and not consider their limited resources.

Jesus would always prove His supremacy over money by pushing us beyond our limited resources so as to completely trust in Him.

In God's order of things, money is our errand runner and not the other way round. I am truly grateful to God for this great deliverance. Therefore, you can now agree that if you run errands for money, you have gone against God's order, and will suffer for it ultimately.

You don't need money, but money needs you. Money needs you in order to gain importance or relevance as an entity.

Prayer Point

Father in the Name of Jesus, we are eternally grateful for exposing us to this great light concerning money. Help us appropriate this truth in our everyday lives Lord, in Jesus' precious Name, Amen.

CHAPTER EIGHT

A WORD TO PARENTS

A brother shared with us recently how he watched his neighbor, an elderly woman wake up as early as 8:00am to play numbers at a nearby sport betting kiosk. Worst of it all was that she was tying a wrapper and had obviously not taken her bath. Please tell me what kind of legacy this woman is laying for her children. A legacy of get-rich-quick schemes and insolence. Here's what the Bible has to say about this;

Psalm 37:38

But the willful will soon be discarded; insolent souls are on a dead-end street. (MSG)

The Lord once shared with me how disappointed He is in us parents. We have failed God woefully in handling these precious gifts that God put in our care. Our children have become nothing more than mere trophies that we decorate to show-off to our friends and the world at large. We must repent now, for the time is short. Very soon, these babies will become men and women. Would you really desire for them to chase the exact same things that you are chasing right now?

Parents, please let's teach our children to work. We must not simply assume that they would work on their own, as they can be influenced wrongly. We have to teach them Genesis 2. I have already started teaching my children about the need for them to be productive.

My daughter recently asked me for the book titled "Purpose-driven life". It is actually when you desire to know your purpose in life that you will discover the need to work in line with God's plan for you. Let's stop giving them the impression that the sole reason for getting a degree is to make money. Help them to know that they are going to school to come out and be productive.

Unfortunately, many of us parents were told this same lie when we were growing up. So we ended up living lifestyles that are money-centered. We must repent and consequently stop this lie from spreading to our posterity. Lack of work is killing the world like a slow poison.

I don't have a problem with working and getting paid a salary, but the question is "what am I being paid for?" Are you productive? Yes, you are supposed to be paid after you execute your job, but what is your ultimate motive for collecting this money? You are paid, but for what?

Please don't misunderstand me. I'm not saying that our children shouldn't work and be paid. A doctor for example is employed to save lives, which is productive. A banker helps people keep their money safe. A carpenter is productive, and the same goes for many countless jobs not mentioned.

The point is to do something to get paid. Encourage them to contribute positively with their hands to the well-being of the society.

In addition to instructing our children aright, we can put a stop to this madness by engaging fervently in prayers for ourselves and our children. Let this revival start with you. Yes you, as you read these words.

Prayer Point

Jesus, You are always interceding on our behalf. The time has come to start praying our youths into their prophetic destinies. Therefore in the Mighty Name of Jesus, we decree an end to purposeless living amongst our youths worldwide. Furthermore, we embrace Your help to be godly parents and guardians to our youths, in Jesus' Most Holy Name we pray, Amen.

KINGDOM ADVANCEMENT

Matthew 6:33

But seek first the kingdom of God and His righteousness, and all these things shall be added to you. (NKJV)

Seeking first God's kingdom and His righteousness is the essence of living as God's child. Hence, the term **"Kingdom**

Advancement" represents activities engaged in propagating the establishment of God's will and purpose on the earth. Therefore, when we engage in kingdom advancement prayers, we are assumed to be praying for the establishment of God's will on earth as it is in heaven (Matthew 6:10).

Having done all these in truth and in spirit, all the things that unbelievers die to have, are added unto us as rewards from a good Father (Hebrews 11:6b).

That being said, I would like us to sit here a bit. Let me continue by asking this question. Child of God, whose kingdom are you really advancing when you engage in these activities? God's kingdom or yours?

Oxford Dictionary defines the word "Kingdom" as **"a realm associated with or** *regarded as being under the control of a particular person or thing."*

Many of us have kingdoms set up in our hearts, which are not under the control of God. We have made up perfect kingdoms in our hearts that consist of the things we desperately desire. So we engage in kingdom advancement activities such as evangelism, outreaches and prayer for souls, with the ultimate aim of advancing the kingdoms we have built in our hearts. Kingdoms that are fully under our control. Kingdoms where everything we ever desire is granted, whether God approves of it or not. A kingdom where I have that perfect car, house, husband, wife, child, house(s), job, money and so on.

When we pray, *"Father, let Your kingdom come and Your will be done..."* 99% of believers are actually thinking about their self-created kingdom, their own perfect world. Even when we are praying the right prayers with our lips, where are our hearts per time?

I must ask myself sincerely, why am I praying kingdom advancement prayers? Is it so that I may end up being settled maritally or to gather possessions? Is my ultimate motive for praying these prayers truly for God or for me?

This is so dangerous because it will lead a lot of people to hell if not taken care of.

Matthew 15:8

'These people draw near to Me with their mouth, And honor Me with their lips, But their heart is far from Me. (NKJV)

If a person's prayers are not for God's kingdom, then it means that he/she is not even a part of His kingdom. At the end of the day, the person will not be raptured. This is not our portion in Jesus' Mighty Name.

God's kingdom advancement is rich work while advancement of a self-created kingdom is poor work. Even the devil had his own kingdom advancement agenda. This is why he was cast out of heaven.

Isaiah 14:12-14

"How you are fallen from heaven, O Lucifer, son of the morning! How you are cut down to the ground, You who weakened the nations! For you have said in your heart: 'I will ascend into heaven, I will exalt my throne above the stars of God; I will also sit on the mount of the congregation On the farthest sides of the north; I will ascend above the heights of the clouds, I will be like the Most High.' (NKJV)

Check your heart and always ensure that it is God's kingdom that you are advancing and not your own.

Charles H. **Spurgeon Quote**: *"A time will come when **instead of shepherds** feeding the sheep, the Church will have clowns entertaining the goats."*

Why did Charles use the term "goats" for Church members? I believe it is because goats are stubborn and they simply love having their own way. They would listen to clowns that entertain them rather than true shepherds who would reprimand their misbehavior.

Spurgeon spoke about this many years ago and it has become a reality in the Church today. We all clap and laugh while motivational speakers pamper us with sweet talks. Then we enjoy so much wealth as a result of chasing our self-created kingdoms.

As far as most denominations are concerned nowadays, if you are rich, then you must be a true Christian. One that understands supernatural things and whom Matthew 6:33 is speaking for. If you are poor however, there must be something wrong with you spiritually.

Beyond financial breakthroughs, various other types of miracles have become something to brag about. You can hardly ever chastise a believer that, *"has it all."* Anyone that is still believing God for one particular miracle or the other is tagged a weak Christian or even an unbeliever. Such a person is believed to lack the kingdom prowess of Matthew 6:33.

Please how many of these things did Anna have?

Luke 2:36-38

And there was also a prophetess, Anna, the daughter of Phanuel, of the tribe of Asher. She was very old, having lived with her husband seven years from her maidenhood, And as a widow even for eighty-four years. She did not go out from the temple enclosure, but was worshiping night and day with fasting and prayer. And she too came up at that same hour, and she returned thanks to God and talked of [Jesus] to all who were looking for the redemption (deliverance) of Jerusalem.

(AMP)

Would you call her a kingdom failure or success? Someone might say, she could have chosen to live a more prosperous life like our Father Abraham. I agree. But just like Anna, Father Abraham did not chase after these things, God was his focus throughout. He obeyed God every step of the way until death.

Can we say this about today's believer? At the end of the day, only God knows those who are His.

2 Timothy 2:19

But the firm foundation of (laid by) God stands, sure and unshaken, bearing this seal (inscription): The Lord knows those who are His, and, Let everyone who names [himself by] the name of the Lord give up all iniquity and stand aloof from it. (AMP)

The devil does not have a problem if you are advancing your own kingdom. He doesn't mind you not advancing his own kingdom either, but will never want you to advance God's own. One great lie that the enemy has sold to many Christians is this; *"Just keep advancing your own kingdom."*

For unbelievers, satan makes some of them advance their personal kingdoms, while others advance his kingdom.

Who is now truly advancing God's Kingdom?

Which Kingdom Am 1 Advancing?

What is the litmus test for identifying which kingdom I am advancing as God's child? The answer is in Matthew 6:33.

1. Blessings chase you.

When blessings and miracles which you never prayed for, begin to appear non-stop in your life, it is a sign that you are advancing God's Kingdom and not yours. This is not to say however, that the poor are sinners destined for hell.

Hebrews 11:6

But without faith [it is] impossible to please [him]: for he that cometh to God must believe that he is, and [that] he is a rewarder of them that diligently seek him. **(KJV)**

To enjoy the blessings of Matthew 6:33, we must believe that God is a rewarder of men, and not a user.

2. Your Focus is NOT on the Blessings.

Another way to be sure that you are advancing God's kingdom, is that the reward is not your focus. You hardly take note of the blessings because you are so consumed with doing more and more in God's heavenly agenda.

3. Passion for souls.

God's number one passion is the souls of men.

2 Peter 3:9

The Lord is not slack concerning his promise, as some men count slackness; but is longsuffering to us-ward, not willing that any should perish, but that all should come to repentance. **(KJV)**

An undying passion for the souls of men, with a burning desire to see them saved and established in God's kingdom, is a sure sign that you are advancing God's Kingdom and not your own.

Sadly, many of us are not truly following our spiritual leaders. This is mostly because we don't know their personal stories. The only part of their stories that interest us is their possessions. For example, we are more intrigued by the private jets owned by them, than by their spiritual growth, battles and how they conquer. We are not after their personal encounters with God and their heart for God's will.

So rather than follow their story, we follow their possessions. That is why many of us are stuck spiritually, remaining babies when we should be mature. (Hebrews 5:14). Deliverance has come for us today in Jesus' Name.

I know of a young pastor, who attempted to reach Bishop David Oyedepo, to invest financially in his ministry. He needed funding basically. It is obvious that this young pastor never followed Papa Oyedepo's story, rather he followed his possessions. Is it any surprise that rather than give him money, God's servant would teach him faith? Because he never borrowed from any man to build God's tabernacle, or fund any Church project. In fact, he sees it as an insult to God Almighty. Should it surprise us that Bishop Oyedepo would turn such an offer down? He would rather sit you down and tell you his story, than give you handouts.

Guess what? He even once turned down a huge amount of money that someone gave him to fund the Church project. He rather asked to learn how to work, than to collect and keep collecting cheap handouts.

Church leaders should please stop making God look cheap. Churches are ordained to be channels of financial fortune to the world, not glorified beggarly institutions. Let's please wake up and be responsible to God and humanity by engaging in rich work.

Psalm 34:10

The young lions lack food and suffer hunger, but they who seek (inquire of and require) the Lord [by right of their need and on the authority of His Word], none of them shall lack any beneficial thing. (AMP)

Inquiring of God and requiring Him as a necessity is rich work. He reveals deep secrets to those that seek Him, including that of financial abundance.

Some of us might be thinking, *"But Daddy Oyedepo has done all the work, why must I work?"* This is a pitiable mindset.

2 Thessalonians 3:10

For while we were yet with you, we gave you this rule and charge: If anyone will not work, neither let him eat. (AMP)

2 Thessalonians 3:11-12

*And now we're getting reports that a bunch of lazy good-for-nothings are taking advantage of you. This must not be tolerated. We command them to get to work immediately--no excuses, no arguments--and **earn their own keep.***

(MSG)

We must inculcate the attitude of earning our own keep in this Kingdom. This was Paul's attitude, and his ultimate reason for great exploits.

Pastor E.A. Adeboye, the General Overseer of the Redeemed Christian Church of God, has shared countless experiences of his somewhat "extreme" personal sacrifices. On one occasion, his dentist told him that his teeth were getting too weak because he was hardly chewing food. According to the dentist's report, he was fasting too much.

Daddy G.O said that he wasn't ready to change his fasting routine for fear of losing his teeth. Just like Esther, he said *"if I perish, I perish"*. To the glory of God, Daddy testified that God renewed his teeth, even with the extreme fasts, to the amazement of his dentist. Is it a surprise that his Kingdom exploits are insurmountable?

It's important to follow people's stories and not their possessions because therein lies deep secrets of benefit to our own lives.

By God's special grace, my family is blessed with an enviable house and a few comforts of life. My husband and I started from renting a very small apartment where we had to share a toilet and bathroom with another apartment. We grew gradually into the current blessings we enjoy.

Everyone has a path that they must follow to get to the top in life. No one can pass through your refiner's fire for you.

Malachi 3:3

He'll take his place as a refiner of silver, as a cleanser of dirty clothes. He'll scrub the Levite priests clean, refine them like gold and silver, until they're fit for GOD, fit to present offerings of righteousness. (MSG)

Bishop David Oyedepo once shared his experience of fasting for so long that he started coughing out blood. He was so weak that he had to crawl down from the prayer mountain on his buttocks. Now some pastors believe that it is not necessary to go to that extreme, because the Bishop has already done it for us. This is a lie that has kept many stuck in mediocrity for too long.

Jesus Christ is the only One who has done everything for us. Bishop Oyedepo is not Jesus Christ, he is a child of God like you and me. What differentiates him from others, is his dedication to God's Kingdom agenda.

We must awaken to our individual responsibility as God's faithful children. If you dodge any trial in one way, it will wait for you in another way. If you dodge any period of fasting that is meant to push you to your next higher level, you will face it in future.

Matthew 17:21

However, this kind does not go out except by prayer and fasting." (NKJV)

Any examination you refuse to write, will wait for you in future until you write it. Examinations of life are not death threats, they are launching pads to our next higher levels.

You must have a lion's heart to obtain a lion's share of God's Kingdom. Don't trade-in your job cheaply on the altar of selfishness, laziness and small-mindedness.

Everyone has his own cross. I can't carry yours and you can't carry mine.

Matthew 16:24

Then Jesus said to His disciples, If anyone desires to be My disciple, let him deny himself [disregard, lose sight of, and forget himself and his own interests] and take up his cross and follow Me [cleave steadfastly to Me, conform wholly to My example in living and, if need be, in dying, also]. (AMP)

Without a cross there is no glory. Rich work is a cross that we must carry, to enter our glorious destinies in Christ. There is no growth without passing through your cross.

Do your own part with utmost dedication, and watch God turn your life around in unimaginable ways.

Prayer Point

Father in the Name of Jesus, cause us to be adequate ministers who are focused on your covenant of grace, which is the fuel for productivity. In Jesus' Mighty Name. Amen.

CHAPTER TEN

THE DEVIL'S LIES ABOUT WORK

As mentioned in the introduction of this book, there are three entities involved in the issue of work. They are;

1. God
2. Man
3. The devil

The mind of God as in relates to work has been well addressed in previous chapters. Man's role as the center piece of this entire mystery has also been largely taken care of. The final and most ignored entity, the devil, will be addressed in this chapter.

The devil will always fight productivity.

1 Corinthians 16:9

For a wide door of opportunity for effectual [service] has opened to me [there, a great and promising one], and [there are] many adversaries. (AMP)

Therefore it is your duty as God's child to fight the fight of faith even while working. Dot not be caught napping on duty lest you be an easy prey of satan and his cohorts.

After we had written our fifth book, the kingdom of darkness unleashed their terror upon our authors and publishers. Excuses for non-delivery started flowing like a flood. There were attacks on the health of publishing team members and even their families. The leader of the team identified the works of the devil, attempting to manipulate completion of projects using the spirit of delay. We entered a session of prayers and fasting and afterwards, a heavy weight was lifted off the team.

Our spirits were revived and the team spirit was restored. Our tasks gained unbelievable traction and speed to the glory of God Almighty.

Matthew 11:12

And from the days of John the Baptist until now the kingdom of heaven suffereth violence, and the violent take it by force. (KJV)

The violent take this Kingdom by force. The devil is no gentleman, so you can't be gentle in your approach to your Kingdom assignment. Principalities and powers are forever against the smooth running of the heavenly Kingdom workflow which you belong. Hence, every task you undertake must be approached with a battle-mode mindset.

The devil will never allow you snatch souls from his kingdom to God's Kingdom without a fight. Therefore we must be ready to fast, pray and always be in right standing with God to manifest a bountiful harvest. The grace is ours already in Jesus' Mighty Name, Amen

Get Rich Quick

When the devil is at work, he never comes straight. One major tactic of the enemy in this generation is *get-rich-quick* schemes. He does this for example, by suggesting a particular side job just to make extra cash. When that extra cash begins to grow above and beyond your regular income, you will most likely drop your work and now start chasing money.

Many parents have ended up training their children not to work to make money. We hear things like *"Child, be smart!"*

One major thing that the enemy stole from man, apart from authority was work and productivity. That's why the old nature is never productive and never giving anything back to humanity. He only knows how to eat endlessly like the Dead Sea. Your body is not created to live like that.

A woman's body is created to conceive and bear children, not a man's own. You must live the way God made you, otherwise, you will suffer for it. If God has created humanity to be productive, that is, to give something, and all you do is just sit and eat non-stop, you've killed yourself already. No one even needs to curse you for your life to be full of woes.

It is only a dead man that is not productive. What we have right now are walking corpses on earth. Everybody is looking at Bishop Oyedepo, refusing to see the work that he does. He owns a private jet, so everyone is striving to own one too.

The devil is so deceptive that he will never come the way you expect.

False Enjoyment

I went to the mall recently and what I saw made my heart break within my chest. Our youths only want enjoyment and no work.

We actually enjoy enjoyment after work. So the enjoyment is not even real when no work has been done. Our youths just want to chill all the time. Please what are they chilling from? They want the same chill mode, from Monday to Sunday.

The Lord said to me, "Get the *Power of a Praying Parent by Stormie Omartian.* You used it to pray for your biological children, now I want you to use it for My youths."

The mall was full and jam-packed with youths, such that there was scarcely any parking space. In fact I think it was only me and my husband that were the oldest people there. At a point we became ashamed that we were even there.

The devil is on rampage with these children and we are sleeping. The devil does not have a problem with the elderly people anymore, his target is our children, because they hold the key to the future.

Of course not all of them are moving about without purpose, but it is only a handful of them that are truly in Christ. Church, what are we doing about this? Or have we left them to their fate, and resigned them to hell forever?

Let us pray for the Lord to turn the hearts of our youths to His truth.

Proverbs 21:1

THE KING'S heart is in the hand of the Lord, as are the watercourses; He turns it whichever way He wills. (AMP)

The youths will never be interested in rich work until their hearts are turned to God. God desires for the youths to turn to Him, but He needs someone to pray. That's part of our work as parents, guardians and elders.

Many people went to that same mall and were not affected in any way. I went and sleep was taken from me. How can I see such and keep quiet in the place of prayer?

For your information, these are your children too. Please do all you can to start praying for them. We must pray until we see a revival in their lives. A revival is all about the working of the Holy Spirit.

Let My People Go

Exodus 9:1

THEN THE Lord said to Moses, Go to Pharaoh and tell him, Thus says the Lord God of the Hebrews: Let My people go, that they may serve Me. (AMP)

Egypt represents a life of sin, slavery and bondage. The Lord made a mighty show of the deliverance of His children from the bondage of slavery. This typifies the deliverance which Jesus wrought for us on the cross, when He made an open show of principalities. (Colossians 2:15).

The sole purpose of your deliverance from the shackles of sin and death is to serve God. Therefore, serving God by engaging in rich work is the key to sustaining your victory over the enemy.

Delay Tactics

Satan is an expert at delaying the works of our hands if we allow him. His tactics include introducing the spirits of laziness, slothfulness, procrastination, excuses and discouragement. He makes us comfortable with non-productivity, and we simply accept it as our fate.

Christians are even comfortable with prayer points like, *"Father in the Name of Jesus, cause the earth to work for Me."* The earth will never work for you because it was never designed to. The earth is only designed to reproduce what has been planted in it. The devil knows this so he keeps his victims stuck in a cycle of ridiculous prayers. We keep praying these prayers that never get answered and we never even bother to ask questions. Some of the answers you seek, you shall find as you read this book in Jesus' Name. And the grace to act accordingly, so as to yield productive results is granted as well.

You must get up and work the earth. This is your job and no one can do it for you, not even God (Isaiah 60). The earth will only yield after you have worked.

It is a beautiful thing to experience God's ultimate master plan for our lives. All we need do is yield to Him according to His Word per time.

It is time for our youths to return to God, but many of them don't know this. This is why we must be fervent on the altar of prayers for their souls. They are the future of Church administration and management.

Do not be weary if you don't see results immediately, only God can turn the heart of any man. Our task is to pray.

When the power and mercy of God comes upon our youths, the scales will fall off their eyes. However, only God knows the time. Your duty is to persist on the prayer altar.

The devil has no power over us than the power we have over ourselves. Simply put, you are more powerful than the devil any day and any time. The devil knows this but will fight our knowledge of this truth.

Hosea 4:6

My people are destroyed for lack of knowledge… (AMP)

Prayer Point

Father in the Name of Jesus, cause a revival to flood the hearts of Your children worldwide. In Jesus' Mighty Name, Amen.

SELF AND WORK

The oldest trick of the enemy is to get humanity to focus on themselves. He knows that any task that focuses on self is poor work, and he has introduced the concept of self-made kingdoms to many believers. For many years, most Christians have blindly gone down this self-destructive path, but this is now being exposed.

When the serpent approached Eve in the garden, he didn't mention anything about his own hidden agenda, or his kingdom (Genesis 3:1-6). He manipulated Eve into focusing on herself, and what she could get out of it. He succeeded in shifting their focus from God's Kingdom to their self-made kingdom.

Genesis 3:6

And when the woman saw that the tree was good (suitable, pleasant) for food and that it was delightful to look at, and a tree to be desired in order to make one wise, she took of its fruit and ate; and she gave some also to her husband, and he ate. (AMP)

According to the above scripture, here is how Eve described her desired, self-made kingdom;

1. Pleasant food
2. Delightful appearance
3. Worldly wisdom

These are the constituents of every self-made kingdom. Let's pause and talk about these three items individually.

1. **Pleasant food:** The flesh always longs to be fed like a spoilt child. All the carnal man cares about is satisfying lustful desires. This is similarly called the *lust of the flesh.*

2. **Delightful appearance:** Sinful appeals become delightful to look at when we are constantly engaged in propagating our self-made kingdoms. This is also known as *lust of the eyes.*

3. **Worldly wisdom:** When the cunning wisdom of the world becomes our focus, we have moved from God's Kingdom agenda. *Pride of life* is reflected in worldly wisdom.

1 John 2:16

*For all that [is] in the world, the **lust of the flesh**, and the **lust of the eyes**, and the **pride of life**, is not of the Father, but is of the world.*
(KJV)

Anytime we contravene God's instruction, we are invariably building self-made kingdoms.

God gave an instruction not to eat of this tree. This instruction represented God's will and purpose for man. This was God's Kingdom agenda. However, man decided to create an agenda for himself which we call a self-made kingdom.

Every time we flout God's agenda, we simultaneously propagate ours. The devil's trick is to always encourage us to propagate our own kingdom. He deceives his victims by reversing Matthew 6:33. Instead of seeking first God's Kingdom, his victims end up seeking their self-made kingdoms first with the hope of propagating God's Kingdom with the returns from their personal agenda. They end up trying to help God. So many Christians make statements like this. "Father please give me that contract, so I can advance Your Kingdom with some of the contract money." This is a fat lie and a death trap. Many have towed this line and have been consumed.

1 Timothy 6:10

For the love of money is a root of all evils; it is through this craving that some have been led astray and have wandered from the faith and pierced themselves through with many acute [mental] pangs. (AMP)

The correct order is to do God's will first and thereafter we obtain the promise. Hebrews 10:36

The promises will end up chasing after you whether you want it or not. The devil knows this and doesn't want you to know it. An end has come to this age-long lie of the enemy in Jesus' Mighty Name.

Sometimes the Lord permits His ordained servants to go their own way until a set time when He snatches them into His own Kingdom. One of my daughters spent many years chasing after money as a chartered accountant. She was financially buoyant, had everything she wanted, but she was empty, sad, broken and suicidal. After some time God snatched her, and now she serves full-time in Watchmaidens Ministry. Rich work enriches, while poor work drains the spirit. This daughter of mine was rich physically but poor spiritually because she was engaged in poor work.

Self-Focus

The devil's major tactic is to turn our attention from God Almighty to ourselves. That's why we keep entertaining excuses for non-performance in God's Kingdom agenda.

How does the enemy achieve this?

He lies to God's children by causing them to shift their priority to filling their pockets first before propagating God's kingdom. In doing this, he reverses the order of Matthew 6:33 in the minds of the gullible, leaving them in the cycle of the world's rat-race forever.

The devil's lies also reverses the impact of what our father Abraham did in his time. Abraham did not wait to fill his pockets after God called him.

Genesis 12:1

GOD told Abram: "Leave your country, your family, and your father's home for a land that I will show you. (MSG)

I have no idea how much father Abraham must have left behind, in obeying God's instruction. It was after he left that God started filling his pockets.

Most of us ask God for permission to do our own thing, before following his instructions. Even right inside the Church while we are praying, we try to arm-twist God to suit ourselves. God will never share his glory with our bank accounts. That is why He would make demands of us that our bank accounts will never be able to meet. In this, our faith muscles are exercised and we please God (Hebrews 11:6). Faith in God is rich work. In fact the only work that is required of us by Jesus, is to believe (John 6:29).

No man can impress God with riches, or the promise to build Churches for Him after He awards us that contract. God is not threatened by our obedience or lack of it. He owns everything including all the money you will ever have. I'm sorry to say this, but God can take care of anything He wants to, without us.

Luke 19:40

But he said, "If they kept quiet, the stones would do it for them, shouting praise."(MSG)

If any child of God refuses to serve God, the stones will do it for him or her. The earlier this truth sinks into our hearts, the sweeter our Christian walk becomes and the freer we are to serve unreservedly.

There is nothing to do *for* God. We are simply privileged to serve humanity *with* God. Amen. Aren't you grateful for this awesome opportunity? It is time for Christians to snap out of the devil's lies and embrace the rich work we must do.

We must make for God first all the time, in order to enjoy Him.

We would never key into God's ordained blessings for us with the mind-set of putting ourselves first, before God. Father Abraham set the pace for us, which pace are you setting for your unborn generation?

Have you ever given a valid excuse for not serving God in certain capacities? You should consider examining your choice in line with this exposed strategy of the devil. He knows the eternal benefits of Kingdom service and will do his utmost best to stop you from serving.

The thief cometh not, but for to steal, and to kill, and to destroy: I am come that they might have life, and that they might have [it] more abundantly. (KJV)

We must guard our Kingdom service jealously and never allow it to be stolen cheaply by the enemy. Therefore, start Kingdom service at your own level, then God will keep expanding the coast of your service.

For example, you don't have to wait to own a car, before taking people to Church on Sunday. Start by paying the transport fare of only one person if that is all you can afford.

Luke 21:1-4

Just then he looked up and saw the rich people dropping offerings in the collection plate. Then he saw a poor widow put in two pennies. He said, "The plain truth is that this widow has given by far the largest offering today. All these others made offerings that they'll never miss; she gave extravagantly what she couldn't afford--she gave her all!"(MSG)

The widow's mite is Christ's acceptable standard of giving and service. I see us being delivered and set free from the lies of the enemy forever in Jesus' Name.

The mindset of grabbing everything for ourselves without engaging in rich work, should be eliminated from the lives of true children of God. The danger of advancing personal kingdom agendas as against God's own, is that it leads to the fate of the rich fool.

Luke 12:16-21

Then he told them this story: "The farm of a certain rich man produced a terrific crop. He talked to himself: "What can I do? My barn isn't big enough for this harvest.' Then he said, "Here's what I'll do: I'll tear down my barns *and build bigger ones. Then I'll gather in all my grain and goods, and I'll say to myself, Self, you've done well! You've got it made and can now retire. Take it easy and have the time of your life!' "Just then God showed up and said, "Fool! Tonight you die. And your barnful of goods--who gets it?' "That's what happens when you fill your barn with **Self** and not with **God.**" (MSG)*

When you decide to engage in God's rich and productive work, self is taken care of.

Prayer Point

Father in the Name of Jesus, we raise a standard of the Blood of Jesus against the power of the enemy over our lives and minds. The yoke is broken forever, and we are free to work in Jesus' Might Name, Amen.

CHAPTER TWELVE

THE WORK OF A HELPMEET

Genesis 2:18

Now the Lord God said, It is not good (sufficient, satisfactory) that the man should be alone; I will make him a helper meet (suitable, adapted, complementary) for him. (AMP)

This is one scripture that gets most Christian women rolling their eyes. It seems like the women are always blamed for every negative happening. From the beginning, even Adam blamed his mistake on Eve.

Genesis 3:12

And the man said, The woman whom You gave to be with me--she gave me [fruit] from the tree, and I ate. (AMP)

Today, women have evolved and become more mentally, psychologically and spiritually advanced than the male gender. From time immemorial, women have taken responsibility where they see men slacking.

For example, so many women have become the bread winners in homes, not because they want to, but because they feel they have to. Unbelieving women are not expected to behave otherwise, because it is assumed that they don't know any better. The sad reality is that Christian women have towed the same line.

As a woman, the only thing that happens to you when we take the place of a man, is hardness of heart. We say that the men have become more and more animalistic, thinking only about food, money and sex; but the same can be said about the women as well, who have also become hardened, thinking only about power.

What does the Bible say about all this? Surely God must have a redemptive plan for humanity, right?

Genesis 2:18

GOD said, "It's not good for the Man to be alone; I'll make him a helper, a companion."
(MSG)

As women, we must understand our roles in the lives of our men. Everything God created was meant to solve a problem, but the enemy will never let us see things in God's perspective. From the scripture above, it is very clear that men are in need of a helper. It is only a deeply spiritual man that would know and accept this truth because the average man sees the woman as a tool, not a helper.

From the moment Adam ate the forbidden fruit, he started seeing the woman as separate from himself. Therefore, we should never expect the man to fully accept his need for a helper.

A sister once shared with us an experience she had with her husband. She said that on one occasion, he offended her terribly and she went into a sulky mood. One day into her grudge, she summoned up courage to lay bare her ill feelings with him. This was how he responded;

"My dear, you know you are our mother. Imagine holding a grudge against our six-year old son because he was naughty, how would he cope without your love?"

The response diffused every anger in her, and she quickly forgave and released herself into loving her husband and family in God's light.

As women, we must understand that the enemy will always fight against God's pure love. This is not about right or wrong, but about spiritual reality. Therefore, your work as a woman is primarily spiritual.

In the eyes of the world, it is allowed for the woman to fight for her right and even walk out on an unfaithful man, but this is not so in Christ.

John 16:12

"I still have many things to tell you, but you can't handle them now. (MSG)

Many of us cannot handle the truth, because it takes dying to self to accept and run with it.

Jezebel Versus Abigail

We have become so accustomed to the fact that Jezebel was evil. But was she not submissive towards her husband? Let's take a close look at the scripture;

1 Kings 21:5-7

Jezebel his wife came to him. She said, "What's going on? Why are you so out of sorts and refusing to eat?" He told her, "Because I spoke to Naboth the Jezreelite. I said, "Give me your vineyard--I'll pay you for it or, if you'd rather, I'll give you another vineyard in exchange.' And he said, "I'll never give you my vineyard.'" Jezebel said, "Is this any way for a king of Israel to act? Aren't you the boss? On your feet! Eat! Cheer up! I'll take care of this; I'll get the vineyard of this Naboth the Jezreelite for you."(MSG)

From verse five, we see a woman who showed concerned about her husband's welfare. We see a woman who is attentive to the feelings of her husband. But why does the Bible call her evil?

Revelation 2:20

"But why do you let that Jezebel who calls herself a prophet mislead my dear servants into Cross-denying, self-indulging religion? (MSG)

In God's eyes, the work of a helpmeet is to help the man to obey God. This is so deep and hidden that it is easy to miss, because that is exactly what the enemy wants women to keep missing.

As a woman, if your husband is a failure, sadly, you are one too. God has put in every woman, the power to influence the man in any way she desires. Therefore, if the heart of a woman beats for God, she will influence her husband to obey God. On the contrary, if her heart beats for herself, she would never be satisfied no matter what the man does. That is why so many women are sad and frustrated.

ABIGAIL

1 Samuel 25:23-26

As soon as Abigail saw David, she got off her donkey and fell on her knees at his feet, her face to the ground in homage, saying, "My master, let me take the blame! Let me speak to you. Listen to what I have to say. Don't dwell on what that brute Nabal did. He acts out the meaning of his name: Nabal, Fool. Foolishness oozes from him. "I wasn't there when the young men my master sent arrived. I didn't see them. And now, my master, as GOD lives and as you live, GOD has kept you from this avenging murder--and may your enemies, all who seek my master's harm, end up like Nabal! (MSG)

Similarly, Abigail was a very submissive wife. With her divine wisdom, she protected her husband Nabal from being killed by David. She interceded on his behalf in line with God's definition of a helpmeet.

1 Samuel 25:32-34

And David said, "Blessed be GOD, the God of Israel. He sent you to meet me! And blessed be your good sense! Bless you for keeping me from murder and taking charge of looking out for me. A close call! As GOD lives, the God of Israel who kept me from hurting you, if you had not come as quickly as you did, stopping me in my tracks, by morning there would have been nothing left of Nabal but dead meat."
(MSG)

Unlike Jezebel however, Abigail's heart was after God. That is why she was able to influence David to obey God and not shed blood. We must learn from this wise woman and start operating the kind of godly wisdom that she did.

After her husband, Nabal died, David immediately asked for her hand in marriage. God never allowed her to suffer the pains of widowhood.

Isaiah 64:4

Since before time began no one has ever imagined, No ear heard, no eye seen, a God like you who works for those who wait for him.
(MSG)

God works full-time for those who wait for Him, I mean those whose hearts honor God. The benefits of trusting God to fight for us as women, in our offices, and as helpers, are boundless. We must learn to let go and let God. Do your part as a helper, and allow God to avenge every disobedience concerning you.

2 Corinthians 10:6

And having in a readiness to revenge all disobedience, when your obedience is fulfilled.
(KJV)

It is only on the grounds of complete obedience that will God fight our battles. I pray that every woman reading this book receives the grace to obey God and trust Him completely in Jesus' Name, Amen.

I was at a Christian meeting some time ago, and of course it was predominantly women that were in attendance. The issue of praying for our men came up, and it ended up being a heated debate. Sadly, I witnessed firsthand as Christian women gloated over their superiority over men.

Men are obviously more in need of help than women, so we must humble ourselves as women, lest we become Jezebels. Any time we find ourselves circumventing God's agenda to help the men, we have become Jezebels. Men are the likely victims and this is impossible for the carnal woman to see.

Romans 12:2

Don't become so well-adjusted to your culture that you fit into it without even thinking. Instead, fix your attention on God. You'll be changed from the inside out. Readily recognize what he wants from you, and quickly respond to it. Unlike the culture around you, always dragging you down to its level of immaturity, God brings the best out of you, develops well-formed maturity in you. (MSG)

This is what is expected of us as women, and this is the rich work of a helpmeet.

Every mature Christian woman knows that her husband needs her prayers to fulfill destiny.

The unfortunate state of most men right now in terms of bondage to sin, laziness, cowardice and all manner of shamefulness, should make a godly woman weep, not gloat. This is the difference between Abigail and Jezebel

Most women have become predominantly competitive. Is this God's original design?

Both Jezebel and Abigail showed physical submission to their husbands, but which of them was doing rich work or poor work in God's eyes? This is the question we must ponder on for spiritual maturity to be achieved.

Abigail and Jezebel were so similar in physical character that only God's estimation told the true story. We would never know that Jezebel was a wicked wife if God had not pointed it out to us in scripture.

The question is, "where is your own heart as a woman?" Is it for God or for yourself? It is only when your heart is for yourself that you would revel over a man's tragedy, no matter the justification.

Matthew 12:30

"This is war, and there is no neutral ground. If you're not on my side, you're the enemy; if you're not helping, you're making things worse. (MSG)

If we are not helping God build the men up, then we are making things worse. The King James Version of Matthew 12:30 implies that we are scattering with the devil if we are not gathering with God.

Our prayer should be for God to help us fulfill His heart's desire on earth concerning our men.

Galatians 3:11

The obvious impossibility of carrying out such a moral program should make it plain that no one can sustain a relationship with God that way. The person who lives in right relationship with God does it by embracing what God arranges for him. Doing things for God is the opposite of entering into what God does for you. Habakkuk had it right: "The person who believes God, is set right by God--and that's the real life." (MSG)

It is obviously impossible to be a helpmeet by brute force. Only God's Spirit can achieve this rich work in and through us, but we must surrender our wills to Him.

Many women do not yet understand the implication of not helping the men, this is why this book is written to open our eyes to the dangers of leaving our tasks undone. The reason Jesus came, is to show us the way of salvation. If we keep insisting on right and wrong, we have missed the point of the cross of Jesus.

A Woman's Primary Assignment

Before closing this chapter, let us take note of this important point. Your duty as a woman in the life of every man around you is to help them obey God. Therefore, you don't have to be married to perform the duty of a helpmeet.

You owe every man around you, be it your son, house-help, colleague, brother, pastor, deacon, father, uncle, cousin and so on, a duty to help them.

Every man around you is in need of help, and you don't have to be a man's wife to help him. Look for creative ways to help every man fulfill his God-ordained assignment.

Let's assume for instance you have a boss that is acting in ungodly ways. As a helper, and his employee, you are to help him in line with God's Word.

This is one thing that the female gender need to understand about the male gender. You don't have to be someone's wife to help that person's destiny.

The kingdom of darkness is very much aware of this and is succeeding at sending many souls to hell with their seductiveness. Christian women must therefore rise up to their responsibility, for the revival of male folk worldwide.

If you see a brother in Church for example, that is lazy and does not know how to take his place in life, you must take it up as your assignment. Go on your knees in prayers and advise him one-on-one as you would your own son.

A godly woman is one that helps every man around her to fulfill God's plan. Here is how the Bible describes her;

Proverbs 31:25-28

Strength and dignity are her clothing and her position is strong and secure; she rejoices over the future [the latter day or time to come, knowing that she and her family are in readiness for it]! She opens her mouth in skillful and godly Wisdom, and on her tongue is the law of kindness [giving counsel and instruction]. She looks well to how things go in her household, and the bread of idleness (gossip, discontent, and self-pity) she will not eat. Her children rise up and call her blessed (happy, fortunate, and to be envied); and her

husband boasts of and praises her, [saying],
(AMP)

Summarily, the rich work of a woman is found in the book of Proverbs 31.

Prayer Point

Father in the Name of Jesus, we ask for a fresh revelation of Your life and Your Spirit, even as we engage actively in the work You have called us to do. In Jesus' Name, Amen.

CONCLUSION

BEGIN THE RICH WORK

Genesis 2:2

And on the seventh day God ended His work which He had done; and He rested on the seventh day from all His work which He had done. (AMP)

God rested from all His work of creation and has finished His part in creating all that we need for life and godliness. He is ever waiting for us to align with His finished work as we are propelled by the power of the Holy Spirit daily.

Coca-Cola, for instance, has finished her work by manufacturing and producing a bottle of coke. As consumers, why don't we keep waiting for the company to help us buy coke from the store, open it for us and even feed us with it? We don't wait like that because it is our job. This is how it is with God's work. Although God has given us the gift of salvation, we must still work it out continually till the day of His appearing (Philippians 2:12).

The head of our publishing team once prayed a prayer of thanksgiving saying, *"Father we thank You for writing books through us."* I corrected this statement by saying that God is not the one writing any book. He finished writing all these books since Genesis 2, and all we are doing is tapping into His finished work.

Productivity boils down to you as an individual. Are you ready to begin the rich work, having understood all that it entails as against poor work?

You must begin to think generationally for the sake of your posterity. Father Abraham gave us an inheritance of productive work, not money. This work has sustained us and is still going to sustain us his children for generations to come.

Today, Israel (Abraham's seed) is so productive that she feeds the entire world in several ways.

We have all been blessed with every spiritual blessing in the heavenly realm. What are you doing with your own?

Ephesians 1:3

May blessing (praise, laudation, and eulogy) be to the God and Father of our Lord Jesus Christ (the Messiah) Who has blessed us in Christ with every spiritual (given by the Holy Spirit) blessing in the heavenly realm! (AMP)

Every child of God is blessed individually, and must work at his own blessing individually. You have no reason to covet another man's blessing because yours is given according to your ability. You must therefore work out your blessing until there's nothing more to do, and make sure you leave this world empty.

In Genesis 2. God blessed the earth with gold. But this gold must be mined to see its beauty. That is the work you are called to do. Mine your own gold and give your all, so that when you leave this earth, your work will keep speaking like that of father Abraham.

BRETHREN, IT IS FINISHED. BEGIN THE RICH WORK!

Prayer Point

Father in the Name of Jesus, we decree that we are not merely a part of Your work on earth, but we are partakers of the harvest as well. In Jesus' Mighty Name we pray, Amen.

ABOUT THE AUTHOR

Watchmaidens Ministry is a Christian interdenominational Para – Church Mission organization, based in Lagos, Nigeria. Founded in September, 2011, Watchmaidens has a clear and strong intercessory mandate anchored on the Word of God, and the vision to pray for the body of Christ, "The Church", the Nations of the world, lost souls and the lost in the Church.

To the glory of God, we have thus far been empowered by the grace of God to stand in this intercessory assignment. Now the Lord has birthed yet another book as a baby born out of a deep passion to see Christians who have imbibed meagre kingdom work ethics, restored to the original image of God. A Church without spot or wrinkle.